CREATIVE
BIBLE LESSONS
IN
1 & 2 Corinthians

CREATIVE
BIBLE LESSONS
IN
1 & 2 Corinthians

12 lessons about making tough choices in tough times

MARV PENNER

Youth Specialties

Zondervan Publishing House

A Division of HarperCollinsPublishers
Grand Rapids, Michigan

Creative Bible Lessons in 1 & 2 Corinthians: 12 lessons about making tough choices in tough times

Copyright © 1999 by Youth Specialties, Inc.

Youth Specialties Books, 300 S. Pierce St., El Cajon, CA 92020, are published by Zondervan Publishing House, 5300 Patterson Ave. S.E., Grand Rapids, MI 49530.

Library of Congress Cataloging-in-Publication Data

Penner, Marv, 1951-
    Creative Bible Lessons in 1 & 2 Corinthians : 12 lessons about making tough choices in tough times / Marv Penner.
        p. cm.
    Includes index.
    ISBN 0-310-23094-2
    1. Bible. N.T. Corinthians—Study and teaching (Higher)—Activity programs. 2. Christian education of teenagers. 3. Junior high school—Religious life. 4. High school students—Religious life. I. Title. II. Title: Creative Bible Lessons in First and Second Corinthians.
BS2675.5.P46 1999
268'.433—dc21
                                               99-30189
                                                    CIP

Unless otherwise indicated, all Scripture quotations are taken from the *Holy Bible: New International Version* (North American Edition). Copyright © 1973, 1978, 1984 by International Bible Society. Used by permission of Zondervan Publishing House.

Scripture quotations marked (NLT) are taken from the *Holy Bible,* New Living Translation, copyright © 1996. Used by permission of Tyndale House Publishers, Inc., Wheaton, IL 60189. All rights reserved.

Edited by Sheri Stanley and Tim McLaughlin
Cover and interior design by Jack Rogers

Printed in the United States of America

99 00 01 02 03 04 05 06 / / 10 9 8 7 6 5 4 3 2 1

Acknowledgments

I've been blessed with a wife who understands ministry and has made it easy to follow God's call. Thanks, Lois, for the friendship and freedom you have given me and your consistent encouragement during this project.

Tim, Jeff, and Melissa—you've often shared me with other kids over the years, but you know that you'll always be in a league of your own. Thanks for making home my very favorite place to be.

I'm honored to be part of the Youth Specialties family. You model excellence and generosity in all you do. Thanks especially to my friends on the National Resource Seminar team. Your integrity and giftedness make our times together rich and invigorating.

A special thanks to the team who helped put this project together: to Tim for your encouragement, to Vicki for your patience and grace, to Karla for your timely prodding, and to the many who work behind the scenes. Thanks for using your gifts to bring these ministry tools into existence.

CONTENTS

HOW TO MAKE THE MOST OF THIS BOOK

These old letters still apply today

As today's postmodern adolescents saunter into the third millennium, Paul's letters to the first-millennium Corinthians are still strikingly relevant. As then, so now: Christians still struggle to retain some degree of moral purity in an X-rated culture, still struggle to cultivate some ethical integrity in a values-free world, still struggle to live according to absolute truth in the middle of relativism and confusion. Christians still find themselves in the daily dilemmas of trying hard not resent those who are disagreeable, of trying hard to overcome pain or doubt or temptation, of trying hard to be charitable and generous toward selfish people.

Paul covers all of this, and more, in his pair of letters to Corinth's Christians. He attempts to remedy church problems, explain church practices, and generally whip them into mature and disciplined shape. The apostle even lays down principles for dealing with the gray areas of Christian experience—questions that have neither a right nor wrong answer in all circumstances.

In short, the letters read like they could have been written last week to Christians in Tempe, Louisville, Sioux Falls, Toronto.

But during the course of this century, many voices have interpreted St. Paul in seemingly clear yet inaccurate ways (simplistic interpretations that have unfortunately trivialized much of the diagnosis and cure that the apostle prescribes for then and now). Adolescents have consequently been deprived of the opportunity to learn to think biblically and theologically about issues with no easy answers. Which is a pity, for Paul tackles his varied and controversial subjects with outspoken conviction, principled clarity, and a strong pastoral flavor. He writes with the gentleness of a mentor and friend. Kind of like a youth worker talking to kids.

The sessions in *Creative Bible Lessons in 1 & 2 Corinthians* reflect the reality of at least the kids I work with and teach, and in ways that (again, to me and my students) are biblically sound, creative, and relevant. What I *don't* do is conclude with authoritative answers matters that St. Paul leaves ambiguous. There's still plenty of tension here between biblical instruction and cultural realities, *so go ahead and allow your kids to wrestle with it.* Don't give in to the temptation to jump in and give them easy answers—the black and white, the superficial, the legalistic. Give your students the time and space to think. Allow them to speak.

And don't you feel pressured to wrap up the lessons in neat little packages of Correct Answers. The tough truths of the Corinthian letters just don't let you wrap them that way.

How the sessions are put together

Tough Times, Tough Truth, Tough Choices doesn't just describe the spirit of Paul's two letters to Corinth, but also provides a logical and convenient outline for each of the 12 sessions. Here are the six components that appear in every session:

• **Here's the Deal** states the purpose of the specific lesson in one concise thought.

• **The Big Picture** offers historical, cultural, or biblical background, putting the sessions into its historic and contemporary context. It points out the larger biblical context of the lesson at hand and the relevance of the lesson to your kids' current cultural context.

• **Just for Starters** are creative ways to funnel students into thinking about the lesson. After all, each student in the room is coming from a very different place emotionally, spiritually, and relationally—which means your first task is to get them all moving in a similar direction. It's a critical burden these activities carry, so choose and plan them deliberately. Neogothic Tess is fresh from a fight with her mom about the black pants, top, and makeup she put on for the evening...Steve is slouched in the back of the room—he just found out he didn't make the team...up in the front row, Taylor is feeling guilty about what happened with her boyfriend last night...tipped back in his chair, Mark is there only because, as usual, he has to be...there's that new girl on the right with a J name, Jessica or Jennifer or something, you forget it exactly, you're glad she's quiet. Only problem is, behind the apparent dutifulness, she's worried about tomorrow's chemistry exam and feeling that she should really be home studying.

Your job is to gather up all that diversity, bring them out of their pasts and futures into the present, and introduce a topic that will benefit everyone. No sweat.

Well, that's the goal, at any rate. The generally lighthearted and participatory activities in Just for Starters should invite your students into the open doors of your lesson and set its tone. So pick the more appropriate opener of the two suggested in each lesson—or do them both if your youth group needs more time to ramp up to the lesson and if you have the time to do both. Or use only the main idea of an activity, and use your own ideas or personality to flesh it out.

At the end of each of these introductory activities is a suggested transition you can use to get smoothly from the activity to the actual teaching of the lesson.

• **Tough Times** is a hands-on link between the lesson's Scripture and the kids' own 21st-century lives. "Hey," this section says to your students, "have you noticed that what this dude Paul is writing about in this letter to a bunch of Christians in Corinth a whole lot of years ago is a huge deal today, too?" Your students need to understand the unfortunately ongoing human condition (people, Christians included, are always screwing things up) as well as the timeless truth of the Bible and the corrective and hopeful insight the apostle has, even about your kids' modern dilemmas.

• **Tough Truth** is a pair of Bible-study components in each session: Digging In and Digging Deeper. The first gets students into small groups to get a grip on that lesson's Bible passage and explore the principles that Paul is working with there. Each Digging In study has a reproducible student handout (you'll find each lesson's handouts at the back of the lesson). Your kids will need two things to benefit most from these Bible studies: Bibles (have plenty on hand for kids who don't bring one of their own) and an adult facilitator for each group (although mature student leadership works as long as you take the time to prep them thoroughly).

Digging Deeper goes, well, deeper. And broader, too. Here are Bible-study activities that take students beyond the Corinthian text, to other Scriptures that explain, expand, or reinforce Paul's points in his Corinthian letters. This section gives your kids a taste of what it's like to trace a theme throughout the Bible.

• **Tough Choices** is the *So what?* section—it wraps up the session with a chance for students to personally respond to what they have learned. *So how will the truth-that-my-youth-leader-just-helped-me-explore-and-understand help me?* is the question your kids should have by this time and the question you should guide them into answering. *How will this truth influence my behavior, my relationships, my attitudes, my priorities?* Never end an encounter your kids have had with truth without the *So what?*

In fact, consider adopting this rule of thumb: whenever possible, hold your students accountable for choices they make as a result of your teaching. Maybe it's deciding to ask someone's forgiveness or vowing to pray their way through the Psalms in a month. Whatever your students' decisions, make a point of checking up on them once a week (as an interested and sympathetic friend, not as a cop) and asking how they're doing.

So go jump into 1 and 2 Corinthians with your students, already!

- You don't have to teach every lesson in this book. They stand pretty well on their own (because Paul wrote these two letters fairly topically). Use the lessons that scratch your group where it itches.

- You don't have to teach the lessons in book order. Rearrange them to suit your teaching strategy or your whim.

- You don't have to use all the activities in each lesson. There's more than enough—not to mention the fact you know so well: some activities that are dynamite in some groups are duds with *your* kids. You know your kids, so use only what works with them.

- Remember that it's the Holy Spirit, not you, who leads people into truth. So relax. Enjoy being led by the Spirit in your own discoveries as you prepare, and enjoy watching your kids discover what the Spirit is leading *them* into.

SESSION 1 MY KINDA TOWN

1 Corinthians, 2 Corinthians, Acts 18

Paul's letters to the Corinthians 2,000 years ago still speak directly to our spiritual and cultural issues today.

You'd think the problems and issues facing a Greek city 2,000 years ago would be nothing more than historical curiosities today. Wrong! Sneak a peek at the letters to the Corinthians and you'll find Paul carrying on about divorce, dating non-Christians, and partying. Sounds familiar, huh? Ancient Corinth was surprisingly similar to our own cities and neighborhoods. What was true for the Corinthians is true for us: the advice and life-guiding principles that Paul wrote to the Christians in Corinth are still relevant 20 centuries later. And the closer attention your kids pay to these letters of Paul, the better prepared they will be to respond to the pressures, demands, and needs of their own community.

OPTION 1 Landmark Artists

Before your students arrive, draw some simple pictures of famous city landmarks on full sheets of paper. We've given some suggestions to get you started. Keep them simple so you don't dampen their desire to participate.

As kids arrive give them several sheets of paper and some markers. Invite them to draw some of their own landmark pictures of places they know. Help them with suggestions if they seem to be drawing a blank (Cinderella's Castle, Statue of Liberty, Empire State Building, or some local landmark most students

continued
on page 14

Remember that when you read these letters of Paul to the Christians at Corinth, you're reading someone else's mail.

Hold it, buster. We're talking about the Word of God here, right?

Uh, right...so you're saying you want me to unwrap that statement a little?

Darn tootin'.

Okay. Let's start here: these English-language documents we call "1 & 2 Corinthians" are letters.

That the same as epistles?

Yup. Epistles, letters— they're all the same. And to whom did he address these letters?

Well, lemme look here at the start of the first letter...uh, "To the church of God in Corinth, to those sanctified in Christ Jesus and called to be holy, together with all those everywhere who call on the name of our Lord Jesus Christ."

Very good. (Really, you have a fine reading voice.) Apparently Paul wrote specifically to the Corinthians—*that* much is clear from the *very* specific church problems he points out later in the letters—but he also knew that his letter would probably be passed around the province some. In fact— look here—the apostle addresses 2 Corinthians to

You'll need...

- sketches of landmarks described in Option 1
- paper
- markers
- tape or tacks for posting artwork

would recognize). Number the creations and post them around the room. Let students guess both what the drawings are and what city they're from.

OPTION 2 Landmark Artists Pictionary

Play this game like the old favorite Pictionary using the cards you've cut up from the **Landmark Artists** page. Divide the kids into teams, and have a timed competition with kids taking turns drawing pictures for their teams to guess.

You'll need...
- cards cut from **Landmark Artists—**Starters 1.1
- flip chart
- markers
- timer or watch

OPTION 3 Weird City Names

Distribute copies of **Weird City Names** and ask your students to identify which eight of the 12 are names of actual North American towns or cities. (Bozo, Funky, Bingo, and Busy are the impostors.)

You'll need...
- copies of **Weird City Names—**Starters 1.2
- pencils

Regardless of the opener you chose, transition into the **Tough Times** section by saying—

More than likely, all of the cities we've just looked at are very similar to each other. There are believers in every one of them. Some of the communities have lots of churches with great leadership and awesome buildings. Others have small struggling groups meeting in humble circumstances.

We're starting a series of lessons today based on a couple of letters written to a group of believers in a particular city nearly 2,000 years ago. Now some of you are already thinking, "Great, what does 2,000-year-old mail have to do with me?" But, I think you'll be amazed at the relevance this mail has to your life today.

The two letters we'll be studying over the next few weeks were written by a guy named Paul, to a church in the city of Corinth—an important city in the Mediterranean in ancient times. Paul cared deeply about his friends in Corinth because he had helped them set up their church while on a trip through the area several years earlier. After a few years, Paul felt they needed a wake-up call, and the letters we find in the Bible are Paul's attempt to get this church back on track.

"the church of God in Corinth, together with all the saints throughout Achaia." There's the province!
You're sure spending a lot of time explaining a few words.
Funny how Bible study does that to a person... Anyway, all that to suggest this: before you have any business asking, "What does this verse or passage or book—
Or word.
—or word mean to me?" before you ask that, the first step in Bible study is asking, "What does this verse or passage or book—or word—mean to whom it was originally written?"
Sounds like I have to be an anthropologist, or at least a historian, before I can hear God speaking to me from his Word.
Well, no. Thank goodness that God can use just about *everything*, and doesn't require *anything*, to start reeling people in toward his heart. Go figure. But sometimes, for some people, a little Bible learning can keep them from goofy ideas, faulty assumptions, false conclusions, and just plain silliness about God. And the thing about believing silly things about God is that it can get ugly quick. It's happened before, and it'll happen again.
Let's not let it happen to us.

Sounds Too Familiar

Move your students into groups of three or four and give each group a Bible, a pair of scissors, and a copy of **Sounds Too Familiar.** Ask them to cut out the headings, the Scripture passages, and the issues from the sheet, then look up each Scripture passage and match it with the appropriate issue. Then ask them to consider our world today and place each paired passage and issue under one of the three headings.

After they're done say something like—

You'll notice that the church today still struggles with most of the issues Paul addresses in this letter. That's why it's so important for us to know and understand Paul's instructions to his friends in Corinth. When God put the Bible together he knew that even 2,000 years later we'd be able to use this advice to live our lives more effectively.

You'll need...
- copies of **Sounds Too Familiar**—Tough Times 1.3
- scissors for groups of three or four
- extra Bibles

DIGGING IN   Active Learning

Acts 18

This section will help students learn about the city of Corinth and the culture of the people there. Use the FYI facts below to put together a short geography-history lesson on the city and what it was like to live there. You might want to do some additional research on your own. A good study Bible or Bible dictionary will have some valuable information. If you have several copies of these kinds of resources available, bring them to class and allow your students the joy of discovering some of the information on their own.

You'll need...
- copies of **C'mon over to Corinth!**—Tough Truth 1.4
- pencils
- flip chart
- markers

FYI facts

- Corinth's location on the thin strip of land (called an isthmus) meant that it had two seaports—one at each edge of the city. For east-west sea traffic and north-south land traffic, it was a true crossroads city.
- In 146 BC the city was leveled by the Romans when the Greeks living there revolted against the Roman government.
- In 46 BC the city was completely rebuilt—that's about 100 years before Paul arrived. In those short 100 years (it took a long time to build a city in ancient times) the population had exploded to about 500,000 people.

- A kind of "marine railroad" was built to haul smaller ships over land from one port to the other. If the ship was too big, its cargo would be hauled over and put on another ship to continue its journey across the Mediterranean Sea.
- Because Corinth was on two major trade routes, the population of the city was more diverse than almost any other city in the Mediterranean. Cultures from every corner of the known world were represented there. The high traffic through the area meant that people who heard the gospel at Corinth could take it back to where they had come from—a very cool strategy by which God saved Paul a lot of traveling.

- Corinth was a city committed to entertaining its people—a huge stadium to host the Corinthian games, the temple of Aphrodite with its 1,000 prostitute-priestesses, many theaters, and a flourishing nightlife of dance, music, food, and drink. It was a party kind of place.
- To "live like a Corinthian" was slang in those days for having no standards or morals.
- Corinth was rattled by two huge earthquakes in 1858 and 1928. Most of the ancient architecture was destroyed. The population of the city today is about 30,000.

Taking it down a notch

For younger students who would enjoy a hands-on experience, this exercise will help them get a feel for Corinth and its strategic location. Use paper mâché and poster paints to make a relief map of the geographical area where Corinth was located. Display the map in the classroom as a reminder that the events being discussed in the Bible happened to real people in real places.

Give each student a pencil and a **C'mon over to Corinth!** sheet and have them pair up to read Acts 18—a passage describing Paul's original visit to Corinth. Ask them to list any clues the passage gives them about the city, the church, or the people of Corinth, and add the information to the bottom of the handout. After they have written the clues, combine two pairs to make a group of four, and have them take turns reading one entry at a time to each other. For extra fun let them score points for any clue they found that the other pair didn't have on their list.

Finish by letting groups report while you compile a master list of things about Corinth on a flip chart. Finally ask your students what Corinth and your own town have in common.

DIGGING DEEPER Selected Scriptures

You'll need...

- a set of cards cut from **In the Real World**— Digging Deeper 1.5
- pencils

Begin by saying something like—

> God calls his people to live in places that are a lot like Corinth. We've seen already that many of the issues are similar. Your school is a place filled with temptations, struggles, hardships, sin, pain, *and* incredible opportunities to make a difference for Jesus.
>
> Now we're going to look at some Bible passages that talk about what it means to live out our faith in the real world. And we'll see that it's not always easy—as these verses tell us.

Divide your students into four groups (or multiples of four if your group is very large—there should be two to six students in each group), and distribute a card from **In the Real World** to each group. Have each group look up the passage on its card and then answer the three questions listed. (Remind your students that this simple three-question approach to Scripture—What does it say? What does it mean? What does it mean to us (me) today?—is a practical tool to use whenever they open the Bible.)

Pull the group back together and review each passage asking students from different groups to give their thoughts on the three questions. The thoughts in these passages build on one another so have students report in the designated order. You might want to make up a chart with the three questions across the top and the four passages down the side to give your students a visual reminder of what they're learning.

Clip tip

EdgeTV—Edition 22 (Youth Specialties) has a brief sketch called "So You Want to Be a Christian?" that addresses what it means to be a Christian with integrity in the real world. It could be helpful in reminding your students of their responsibility to be Christ's voice in their world.

Hometown Profile

Obtain or create a large map of your own city. You could have students sketch one up on poster board—include major streets and landmarks. For larger groups, divide your students into groups of eight to 10 and give each group a map of its own. Or copy a map onto a transparency and project it on the wall so everyone can see.

Using different colored markers, have the students identify the following regions of your community:

- **Blue:** where people in your community are hurting in some way—hospitals, jails, shelters, or individual homes of people the students know
- **Black:** where sinful or evil things happen in your city—prostitution, crime, violence, gossip, slander, greed, or selfishness
- **Red:** places of temptation for students—school, the corner store, liquor stores, arcades, etc.

Finish by giving students an opportunity to come to the map and draw a star where they feel they could make a difference for Jesus. It could be one of the places that's been marked, or it could be the home of a friend. You might even suggest they put a star at their own home address if they need to make a difference in their family. Have them sign their name to the star. Post the maps around the meeting room for the duration of this series of lessons from Corinthians.

Close in prayer thanking God for students who are willing to make a difference in their own community.

Memorize this promise Jesus gave his friends just before leaving them.

But you will receive power when the Holy Spirit comes on you; and you will be my witnesses in Jerusalem, and in all Judea and Samaria, and to the ends of the earth. (Acts 1:8)

You'll need...

- a large map of your city (see options described below)
- colored markers

Extra effort

After identifying the key areas in your community that need to experience the light of the gospel, consider taking your students on a tour and spending a few minutes of group prayer at each location. It shouldn't be a big public spectacle—just a carload of kids stopping briefly and asking God to give them opportunities to bring his light to the darkness there. And remember to help your students realize that they're not praying for "the place"—they're praying for themselves and the courage they'll need to make a difference in that place.

Landmark Artists

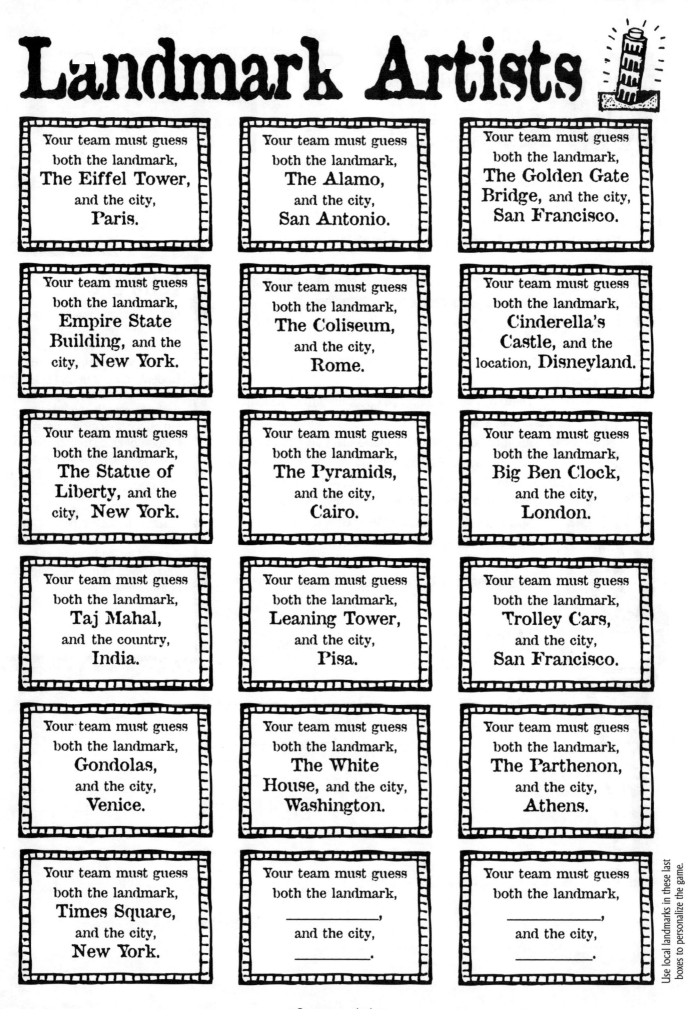

Your team must guess both the landmark, **The Eiffel Tower,** and the city, **Paris.**

Your team must guess both the landmark, **The Alamo,** and the city, **San Antonio.**

Your team must guess both the landmark, **The Golden Gate Bridge,** and the city, **San Francisco.**

Your team must guess both the landmark, **Empire State Building,** and the city, **New York.**

Your team must guess both the landmark, **The Coliseum,** and the city, **Rome.**

Your team must guess both the landmark, **Cinderella's Castle,** and the location, **Disneyland.**

Your team must guess both the landmark, **The Statue of Liberty,** and the city, **New York.**

Your team must guess both the landmark, **The Pyramids,** and the city, **Cairo.**

Your team must guess both the landmark, **Big Ben Clock,** and the city, **London.**

Your team must guess both the landmark, **Taj Mahal,** and the country, **India.**

Your team must guess both the landmark, **Leaning Tower,** and the city, **Pisa.**

Your team must guess both the landmark, **Trolley Cars,** and the city, **San Francisco.**

Your team must guess both the landmark, **Gondolas,** and the city, **Venice.**

Your team must guess both the landmark, **The White House,** and the city, **Washington.**

Your team must guess both the landmark, **The Parthenon,** and the city, **Athens.**

Your team must guess both the landmark, **Times Square,** and the city, **New York.**

Your team must guess both the landmark, _____, and the city, _____.

Your team must guess both the landmark, _____, and the city, _____.

Use local landmarks in these last boxes to personalize the game.

WEIRD CITY NAMES

Some of these cities are bogus, and others are real. Can you tell which are which?

- Pig, Kentucky
- Inspiration, Arizona
- Bozo, Montana
- Moose Jaw, Saskatchewan
- Funky, Idaho
- Security, Colorado
- Bingo, Missouri
- Madonna, Maryland
- Busy, New York
- Ordinary, Kentucky
- Virgin, Utah
- Cool, California

Starters 1.2 Copyright Youth Specialties, 300 South Pierce Street, El Cajon, CA 92020.

Sounds Too Familiar

Just Back Then—Not Right Now

Just Right Now—Not Back Then

Both Back Then—And Right Now

1 Corinthians 1:12	1 Corinthians 5:1	1 Corinthians 3:3	1 Corinthians 6:14-20
1 Corinthians 6:6-8	1 Corinthians 7:10-11	1 Corinthians 8:4-6	1 Corinthians 11:4-6
1 Corinthians 11:20-22	2 Corinthians 6:14-16	2 Corinthians 11:13-15	2 Corinthians 12:7-10
Hats, shaved heads, and hairdos for women	Arguing over which version of the Bible to use	Painful experiences that are hard for us to understand	Body piercing and tattoos
Silly lawsuits and taking other Christians to court	Christians putting each other down—quarreling, not getting along	HIV, AIDs, Hepatitis C from drug abuse and other poor choices	Divorce and remarriage
Sexual abuse within families	Eating food that has been sacrificed to idols	Prostitution and sexual immorality of various kinds	Unhealthy hero worship and the arguing that comes with it
People getting drunk and disorderly when sharing in the Lord's table	Dating or marrying an unbeliever	Abuse of time on the Internet or with video games	Cults and teachers of false beliefs and religions

C'mon over to Corinth!

Tough Truth 1.4 Copyright Youth Specialties, 300 South Pierce Street, El Cajon, CA 92020.

In the Real World

Group 1—2 Corinthians 6:17

What does it say? Summarize the thought of this verse in your own words.

What does it mean? What is the writer trying to say?

What does it mean to me?

Group 2—John 17:15-18

What does it say? Summarize the thought of this verse in your own words.

What does it mean? What is the writer trying to say?

What does it mean to me?

Group 3—Acts 1:8

What does it say? Summarize the thought of this verse in your own words.

What does it mean? What is the writer trying to say?

What does it mean to me?

Group 4—Matthew 5:13-14

What does it say? Summarize the thought of this verse in your own words.

What does it mean? What is the writer trying to say?

What does it mean to me?

 "SESSION 2"

FRIENDS DON'T LET FRIENDS GO UNFORGIVEN

1 Corinthians 5, 2 Corinthians 2:5-11

When accountability gets just plain hard—confronting sin in another believer.

Few personality traits are prized today as highly as tolerance and open-mindedness. Open-minded people, we're told, willingly accept others, their ideas, and their behavior unconditionally, without judging or imposing any moral standard on them. Of course, no one wants a reputation for being close-minded, so we tend to overlook sin in other people's lives. It's none of our business, we reason. (And we secretly hope that others will return the favor by overlooking our sin.)

As you might imagine, Paul had some strong words about this hands-off approach to community ministry. He demanded that the Corinthians point out sin within their church and confront it directly. Unpopular as it may be, that demand still applies today. If your students truly care about their friends, they won't look away when those friends cross the line into sin. Instead, they will learn to speak the truth in love, hold one another accountable, and dare each other to more deliberate godliness.

OPTION 1 Been There, Done That Game

This is one of those one-less-chair-than-people games where your students sit in an open circle with someone left standing in the middle. It illustrates how selective we can be about what we reveal to others.

In this version the person in the middle tells the group something unusual they've done at some point in their lives ("I've gone deep sea fishing," "I've been to Europe," "I've taken eighth grade math three times," etc.) and says "Go." Anyone else in the group who's done the same thing has to get up and move to another chair while the middle person tries to get a seat himself. The easiest way for the person in the middle to get seated is to think of something that some, but just a few, people have done.

FYI

"What business is it of mine to judge those outside the church?" Paul rhetorically asked in his first letter to the Corinthian church. But the Christians in that church had *every* right, he argued, to judge their own *inside* the church. "Are you not to judge those inside? God will judge those outside. Expel the wicked man from among you."

It's passages like this that give Paul something of a severe and brusque reputation to some readers. Though this situation probably justified his point-blank imperative: one of the church members had apparently slept with his stepmother. And Paul didn't cut this guy any slack: "Hand this man over to Satan, so that the sinful nature may be destroyed and his spirit saved" (a verse misused by medieval Inquisitors to justify death sentences they handed down to supposed heretics).

But by the time Paul wrote his second letter to

continued on page 24

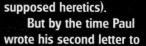

You'll need...

• a circle of chairs (one less than the number in your group)

FYI cont. this church, there seems to have been repentance, forgiveness, and reconciliation (2 Corinthians 2). The punishment the church laid on this man was sufficient, Paul wrote—and now it was time "to forgive and comfort him, so that he will not be overwhelmed by excessive sorrow."

In every church's experience, the time comes (usually more than once) when it must appropriately (and with grief, not with indignation or self-righteousness) confront an individual, call a spade a spade, and expel the person from the church—and then be ready to forgive the person and welcome him or her back into the church with compassion instead of hard feelings.

This game is a safe way for kids to tell each other about themselves without feeling like they're bragging. Play until everyone in the group has had the opportunity to be in the middle. If your group is large, divide into several smaller circles so everyone can participate.

OPTION 2 To Know, Know, Know Me

You'll need...

- poster board sign described in Option 2

Ask your students to think about how they would complete this sentence: "To really understand me, you need to know that..." Copy the phrase onto a piece of poster board large enough for everyone to see as they think about how they would finish it.

Tell your students that you'd like at least one response from each of them, but give them two or three shots if they're willing. Be sure that you participate as well. You'll probably hear things like, "I'm shy in front of people," "I'm the only girl in my family," "I love sports," and so on. If your group is close, they might say things like, "My family is going through a tough time right now," or "I've been questioning my faith lately." Just listen to the responses and acknowledge each one. Remember that self-disclosure is scary at any level for some people. Thank them for sharing with one another.

Blatantly badly dressed

Since this is a lesson on lovingly confronting one another about areas in our lives that need adjustment, this simple object lesson might help. If you have the courage, come to class with a fairly obvious fashion faux pas—your shirt buttoned up wrong, a piece of lint on your shoulder, mismatched earrings, or (if you're a guy teaching guys) your fly down. If someone notices and says something, thank them, make the adjustment, and let it go until later when you make the transition to the **Tough Times** section. At that point you can use it as a positive illustration of the big idea of this lesson.

If no one says anything, you can ask, in your transition, if anyone noticed. If the answer is yes, you've got a great opportunity to remind them of how tough it is to point out things in the lives of others. If no one noticed, remind them that we often don't see the things that should be addressed in others' lives. (Or you might just have to realize that your students are so used to seeing your lack of fashion awareness that they've given up trying to help you.)

Regardless of the opener you chose, transition into the **Tough Times** section by saying—

We just had the chance to let the rest of the group know something new about ourselves (review some specifics). And while some of us were more vulnerable than others, there is still a lot we didn't share.

We didn't hear many people share about their inappropriate sexual thoughts, or the anger they feel toward an individual in the group, or their secret eating disorder or drug addiction. A lot of that stuff stays hidden inside. Interestingly—it isn't always as secret as we wish it was. And when friends see those things, they don't bring them up because they don't want to step on toes or hurt friendships.

Think about what the role of a Christian friend should be when it comes to those types of issues in our lives—the things that must be changed. This lesson will help us understand how to confront the sin we see in others.

Who Me?

Give your students the **Who Me?** list of possible adolescent struggles. Have them put a check mark beside any struggles they've seen in their friends. Then ask—

- Have you ever confronted a friend in one of these areas? Why or why not?
- Have you ever been confronted in one of these areas?
- Without telling us what it was, how did it feel?
- Could the person have done it differently to make it more helpful?

Don't get bogged down on the questions at this point. The discussion is meant to be introductory and to simply point out that we have access to each other's lives at a level where we could make a difference.

DIGGING IN Small-Group Discussion

1 Corinthians 5
2 Corinthians 2:5-11

Distribute pencils and copies of **Digging In: Hey! You shouldn't do that!** To benefit the most from this discussion, your students should each have a Bible as well. Have your students break into smaller discussion groups. If it's possible, have an adult leader with each group. A mature student leader could also facilitate each small group.

This discussion will teach us how we ought to respond when we find that someone in the church is sinning and unwilling to stop.

Taking it down a notch

Help your younger students realize that the most important accountability relationship they may have right now is with their parents. Emphasize the value of demonstrating a teachable spirit when their parents try to help them grow. Be sensitive to the fact that many of them will be struggling with their moms or dads. Encourage them that giving some consideration to the advice of their parents is a step in the right direction.

DIGGING DEEPER Matthew 18:15-17

You'll need...
• plain paper
• pencils

In this passage Jesus gives us some very specific instructions on confronting sin in the life of another.

Pair your students up and have them diagram the steps Jesus instructs us to take when someone sins. Boxes, circles, and arrows might be the kind of visual tools that would illustrate this process. Don't give them too much help on this—you'll be surprised by what they come up with. Have each group explain its diagram. If your group is large, simply have each pair explain its diagram to two other pairs.

Extra effort

Some of your students may be ready for a more structured program of prayer partnerships and mutual accountability. Help them see the value of meeting weekly with a prayer/accountability partner by building it into your youth ministry program.

You could meet at the beginning of the program with all who are interested, teach them how to pray for one another, discuss what appropriate self-disclosure involves, and emphasize the importance of confidentiality in such relationships. Regular meetings (once a month or so) to teach them further lessons on community, integrity, and mutual ministry could be very helpful in keeping them committed to one another. By the way—this will work best if you are in this kind of a relationship yourself.

Quiet Closing

The closing for this session is quiet and introspective. Ask students to return to the list of adolescent vices you gave them in the **Tough Times** section of this lesson. Tell them that the closing is personal—just between them and God.

Ask them to look at the list and identify any issues that exist in their own lives. Then give them a time of quiet personal prayer, encouraging them to acknowledge a need in that area. Finally ask them to consider sharing their area of potential growth with a friend who can hold them accountable. Play the dc Talk song "What if I Stumble?" as suggested in the Clip Tip.

Close in prayer asking God to give students courage to confront the sin in their own lives.

You'll need...
• **Who, Me?** student lists from the Tough Times activity

Memorize this thought from one of Paul's letters.

For you were once darkness, but now you are light in the Lord. Live as children of light. (Ephesians 5:8)

Clip tip

dc Talk has a great cut for closing this session on their *Jesus Freak* (ForeFront, 1995) album. "What If I Stumble?" addresses the importance of Christian community when we fail. Your kids may know it. Encourage them to sing along and listen carefully to the words in light of what they've just learned.

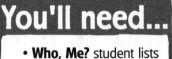

Who, Me?

Do you know anyone who—

- ☐ Cheats at school?

- ☐ Lies to parents or teachers?

- ☐ Drinks or abuses drugs even occasionally?

- ☐ Surfs for pornography on the Internet?

- ☐ Dates an unbeliever?

- ☐ Shoplifts in stores or steals from their parents?

- ☐ Is sexually active in a dating relationship?

- ☐ Gossips and talks behind people's back?

- ☐ Wastes way too much time on video games or the 'Net?

- ☐ Uses a fake ID to get into places they shouldn't go?

- ☐ Uses God's name in vain or tells off-color jokes?

Tough Times 2.1

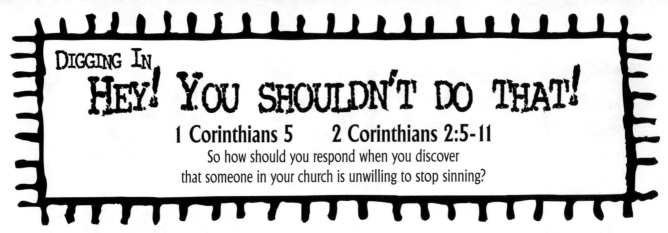

HEY! YOU SHOULDN'T DO THAT!

1 Corinthians 5   2 Corinthians 2:5-11

So how should you respond when you discover
that someone in your church is unwilling to stop sinning?

1. A lot of people outside the church say that Christians are just a bunch of hypocrites. (That means that their walk doesn't match their talk.) Are these people right?

2. What are some examples you've seen of people who are part of a church but live as they please?

1 Corinthians 5:1-5

3. What's the issue Paul is so ticked off about in verse 1?

4. Is there also an attitude Paul is upset about (Look at verses 2 and 6)?

5. According to verse 2, what should we feel when a fellow Christian chooses to make sinful choices?

6. Is Paul being too harsh in his suggested punishment in verse 5?

1 Corinthians 5: 6-8

7. Who knows how yeast works? Explain.

8. Why is yeast a good picture of how sinfulness affects a church?

9. In verse 8 Paul uses some words to describe what the church ought to be like. What are they and how would you define them in your own words?

1 Corinthians 5: 9-11

10. Is Paul saying that we should have nothing to do with anyone who sins or is there a special group of sinners that we should stay away from?

11. Some religious groups forbid their people from having anything to do with outsiders. Why do you think they make such rules?

12. What would happen to Christianity if that were a rule for you?

1 Corinthians 5:12-13

13. What words would you use to describe how Paul is feeling as he writes this?

14. Are we tough enough on sinners in our church?

2 Corinthians 2:5-10

15. Do you sense a different attitude toward this sinner? What's the spirit of these verses?

16. Verse 7 tells us how this guy feels about his sin. How is that different from the one in the 1 Corinthian verses?

17. Some people have wondered if this is the same person that Paul is talking about. Do you think it could be?

2 Corinthians 2:11

18. Why would Satan want us to be unforgiving?

19. How can we know if we should be harsh with sin and kick people out—or if we should be forgiving and give them another chance?

20. What is Jesus' attitude toward people who are sad about their sin?

Tough Truth 2.2

SESSION 3 — YOU'LL HEAR FROM MY LAWYER!

1 Corinthians 6:1-11

HERE'S THE DEAL

With Paul's strategy of conflict resolution, Christians can settle their differences with each other in a God-honoring manner.

THE BIG PICTURE

"Don't take the law into your own hands—take 'em to court," said the announcer on "People's Court." That attitude is now the option of choice for everyone who's ever been wronged in our society. If you've got a beef, chances are you've got a lawyer.

Things weren't much different in first-century Corinth. Members of the Corinthian church, in fact, regularly hauled each other to court to settle their differences. You can imagine the devastating effects these lawsuits had on church unity. To restore and promote fellowship, Paul offered some practical suggestions for resolving conflict outside of the legal system—essentially an early form of Christian arbitration, a strategy that is still relevant today.

Your students should understand that regardless of our differences, Christians are all part of the body of Christ, and consequently united by that powerful common bond. Yes, conflicts between believers are inevitable. But those conflicts should be dealt with in a way that reflects our concern for and commitment to each other.

FYI

Like every city ancient and modern, Corinth had its army of lawyers and collection of courtrooms. Daily business depended on legal decisions then as it does now. But what if both the defendant and the plaintiff in a legal suit were Christians—both of them members of the city's church?

Which was exactly the case that Paul addressed in 1 Corinthians 6: 1-11. And once again, his instruction was both radical and entirely logical: why take a dispute with another Christian to an unbelieving judge? Why submit the church, whose operating system is that kind of love among believers called charity, to the mediation of a court that operates according to the world's system? Certainly, Paul wrote, you should appoint members of your own church to judge a grievance between Christians—and these church "judges" should not be the CEOs and

continued on page 30

JUST FOR STARTERS

OPTION 1 A Scripted Scrap

This opener can be very effective if you have a couple of students who enjoy improvisational drama and can be convincing actors. Get together with them a few days in advance to explain that they'll need to stage an argument in front of the group. The focus of the squabble can be whatever they want, but it should involve one of them in a victim role and the other as an indifferent and defensive perpetrator. Have them start the argument with a hypothetical question to you. See the example script, Starters 3.1.

You'll need...

- two students for an improvisational drama
- **A Scripted Scrap—** Starters 3.1, for reference only

29

End the object lesson by interrupting your players with a simple, "Okay guys, I think that'll do. Shake hands and make up, you're friends again." Explain that the squabble your students just witnessed was staged. Complement them on their ability to make it look real, and remind your students that there are plenty of conflicts between people that are very real.

OPTION 2 You Be the Judge

You'll need...
- copies of **You Be the Judge**—Starters 3.2
- pencils

Give your students pencils and copies of **You Be the Judge**. It contains details of a number of actual lawsuits brought to North American courts in recent years. The idea is for them to determine which of the lawsuits were successful and which were not.

(The blackjack player was the only loser. All the other lawsuits stood up—and paid up—in court.)

Regardless of the opener you used, transition into the **Tough Times** section by saying—

Our world is full of people pointing fingers at each other for all kinds of things. Sadly church youth groups are not immune to the problem. So often in churches, good friends end up fighting and losing their friendships in the process.

It may be true that conflict is an inevitable part of living together. The goal of this lesson is not to eliminate conflict, but to help us know how to biblically resolve conflict when it happens.

FYI cont.

stock brokers and contractors in the church, but people "of little account." The minimim-wage people.

In fact, Paul concluded to the Corinthians, you shouldn't be taking anyone to court in the first place, whether to the civil court or to your own "church court." You ought rather be wronged and cheated than file a grievance against your spiritual brother or sister.

We told you Paul's advice was radical.

TOUGH TIMES

Ya Wanna Duke It Out, Huh?

Have your students briefly brainstorm a list under the following questions. Record their answers on a flip chart.

You'll need...
- flip chart
- markers

- What do friends fight about?
- What do neighbors fight about?
- What do dating couples fight about?
- What do husbands and wives fight about?
- What do parents and teenagers fight about?

Ask them if they see any themes or patterns. They should notice things like selfishness, abuses of power, trivial issues getting blown out of proportion, bad communication, etc.

TOUGH TRUTH

DIGGING IN Small-Group Discussion

1 Corinthians 6:1-11

Explain that this discussion will teach us what to do when we're in conflict with other Christians. Pass out pencils, Bibles, and **Digging In: I'm right, and you're wrong** for this session. Then have your students break into their small groups for discussion. Again, if it's possible, have an adult leader with each group. A mature student leader could also facilitate each small group.

You'll need...

- copies of **Digging In: I'm right, and you're wrong**—Tough Truth 3.3
- pencils
- extra Bibles

Did you know?

The churches in Paul's day followed his instructions. They set up court systems of believers who could deal biblically with people's problems. These courts gained such a reputation for fairness that many unbelievers came to have their disputes settled there. For several centuries church courts were a major part of the justice system. God's ideas work for everyone!

DIGGING DEEPER James 4:1-10

Have groups of three students read the passage in James and then summarize the message in a simple four-line rhyming poem, like this:

> The quarrels you have seem to come from within,
> You claw and you grab and you fight and you sin.
> But God says be humble, come near me and pray,
> I know what you need and I'll lift you today.

When they're finished, bring the groups back together and read the poems aloud.

You'll need...

- plain paper
- pencils
- extra Bibles

Extra effort

Set up a Kangaroo Court with a judge, bailiff, court reporter, and prosecuting attorneys. Bring fun and frivolous charges against kids in the group. For example:

- Tim, you are charged with just being way too happy in the morning. All that smiling and singing you did on the Saturday morning of the retreat before anyone else was out of bed was more than any of us could stand, and we're sick of it! How do you plead?

- Jeff, you are charged with lowering the water in the lake to dangerous levels. Every time you wiped out water skiing last weekend, you sucked back several gallons.

- Melissa, you're charged with exceeding baggage limits. Three duffel bags, a knapsack, and a sleeping bag on the canoe trip...

Set up the room like a courtroom, get a choir robe and rubber mallet for the judge, go through the formal procedures to an extreme, call witnesses, make up section and paragraph numbers from your own criminal code, and have fun with it. Just remember—in the end everyone is guilty and gets sentenced to some kind of fun consequence that can be done right away.

Don't let this exercise hurt kids' feelings or cause pain. Don't attack character or expose things that might be sensitive in any way. Choose consequences that are fun without being embarrassing. Set it up so that kids will be secretly disappointed if they don't get charged with something. Err on the side of kindness. Emphasize creativity rather than cruelty, and keep it lighthearted and safe for everyone.

TOUGH CHOICES

Blessed Are the Peacemakers

Distribute pencils and the top half of **Blessed Are the Peacemakers,** one to each student. When they have completed the exercise, hand out the second half and have them fill in the numbered blanks with the information from the first half. Ask them to consider praying the prayer each morning this week.

You'll need...

- copies of **Blessed Are the Peacemakers**— Tough Choices 3.4, cut in half
- pencils

Clip tip

Videotape a brief case (not a briefcase) from one of the current popular court shows on TV (for example, "Judge Judy"). Be sure to avoid any episodes with inappropriate themes. Stop the tape before the verdict, and let your students decide who's right and why.

Memorize this counsel from Paul's letter to the Ephesians.

Make every effort to keep the unity of the Spirit through the bond of peace. (Ephesians 4:3, NLT)

A SCRIPTED SCRAP

Here's an example of the type of argument your students could act out.

VICTIM: *(to teacher)* Hey, I have a question before we get going today. What would you do if someone who said they were your friend told a lie to your parents and got you into a bunch of trouble?

TEACHER: I guess that would all depend…

VICTIM: *(just carrying on)* You know we talk a lot in here about being good friends and having "community"—about helping each other out…Yeah, right! *(sarcastically with a bit of a sneer)*

PERPETRATOR: *(under his breath and directed toward victim)* It's pretty obvious you're talking about me. Why don't you just go ahead and say my name so everyone will know?

VICTIM: No. No one would have known if you had kept your big yap shut.

TEACHER: Whoa. Hold up there. I thought you guys were friends.

VICTIM: Yeah. *Were* friends is about it.

PERPETRATOR: I can't believe you're doing this. You know you were wrong—and besides, I only told your parents because they asked.

VICTIM: What you told them wasn't even true.

PERPETRATOR: I told them what I saw.

VICTIM: You told them what they wanted to hear. You were just trying to save your own tail and you know it.

The argument should continue along these lines for a minute or two— even escalating to pushing and shoving.

Starters 3.1

You Be the Judge

These are actual lawsuits brought to North American courts in recent years. Which ones do you think actually stood up in court and won?

• A Kansas insurance company employee hurt himself lifting his briefcase out of his trunk. He missed no work, kept playing golf, but sued his company for $95,000 because he had experienced a work-related injury.

• A New Hampshire high school student went up for a slam dunk and caught his teeth on the net as he came down. His parents sued the company that manufactured the net for $50,000.

• An Indiana burglar sued the owner of the house he had robbed. While the crook was making a getaway the homeowner shot him in the behind. The burglar—now in prison for 12 years—complained that his injury made it painful for him to sleep and sit down.

• Inmates at the Salem Massachusetts county jail sued the county sheriff for $2,000,000 because of "cruel and unusual conditions." They complained about multiple bunking and the fact that they had no place to exercise in the winter.

• A California woman sued a Las Vegas casino for the $350,000 she lost playing blackjack one weekend. She claimed that it was the casino's responsibility to tell her she was a lousy card player.

• A California landlord sued the estate of his former tenant who had died. The suit was based on the fact that the tenant had died without giving 30 days notice to the landlord.

• A New Mexico woman sued McDonald's for $2.9 million because the cup of coffee she had bought burned her leg when she tipped it over.

• A Midwest golfer sued his golf course for $85,000 because his badly hit ball bounced off a lamp post and hit him in the face.

From *Presumed Ignorant* by Leland Gregory III (Dell Publishing, 1998).

Starters 3.2

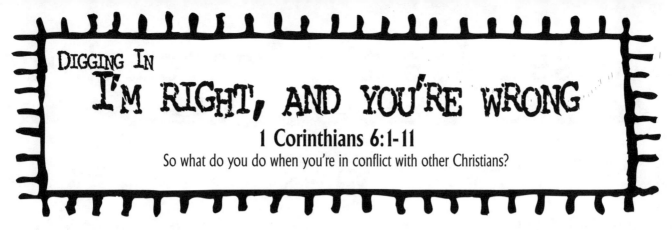

1. Do you think the court system in this country is fair?

2. What are some evidences you've seen to give you confidence in the courts? What are some things that have made you wonder?

3. To whom would you go if you needed help in settling a quarrel with a friend. Why?

1 Corinthians 6:1-6

4. What problem is Paul addressing in verses 1 and 2?

5. What are some issues people in our group fight about?

6. According to verse 4 what is Paul's solution to the problem?

7. Verse 6 makes it sound like Christians should keep their squabbles secret—kind of pretend that everything is okay. Some families are like that, too. Is that what Paul is concerned about?

8. How practical would it be to have a church-based process for people to use if they needed to settle a dispute?

9. Can you think of people in our church qualified enough to be those kinds of judges? (Perhaps elders could serve such a function.)

1 Corinthians 6:7-8

10. The first part of verse 7 is a very strong statement. It seems like this is what he's really upset about. What do you think Paul means by it?

11. In the first part of this chapter, Paul suggests an alternate court system, but now he is making a far more radical suggestion. What is it?

12. Can you think of anything Jesus said that reminds you of this suggestion?

13. How could there ever be justice for victims if we chose to live this way? Wouldn't the weak and quiet people just get abused?

14. How would our group be different if we lived by this suggestion?

1 Corinthians 6:9-11

15. What's up with the long list of sins Paul uses to describe these people in verses 9 and 10? What is he trying to say to them?

16. Why is the first part of verse 11 written in the past tense?

17. *Washed* means that we're clean, *sanctified* means that we've been set apart to serve God, and *justified* means that when God looks at us he doesn't see our faults. How should this description change our attitudes about people who hurt us?

Tough Truth 3.3   Copyright Youth Specialties, 300 South Pierce Street, El Cajon, CA 92020.

Blessed Are the Peacemakers

1. Write down the name of a person you often find yourself fighting with.

2. Write down what you usually fight about.

3. Think of one thing—even a small thing—you could do to reduce the tension.

4. What is one genuine need of the person you wrote down for number 1 above?

Dear Lord, This isn't easy because you know I'm struggling to love

_____ these days. We just can't get along the way
                    1
we should. I know that it's wrong for us to be fighting the way we are,

but it seems like every time we get together it's the same old thing—

_____. I know that if I
                2
_____ it would be
                3
a step in the right direction, but I need you to give me the desire and

the strength to do it. I realize that _____ needs
                                                            1
you to provide_____ and I ask that you would meet
                        4
that need today. I can't do this on my own, so I'm asking you to help me.

In Jesus' name, Amen

Tough Choices 3.4

THOSE PESKY STDs
(SEXUALLY TOUGH DECISIONS)

1 Corinthians 6:13-20

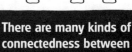

Freedom is the result of making good moral choices for good reasons.

If there's one thing the human race excels at, it's corruption. There's nothing on earth we can't pollute, pervert, or distort. Just look at God's gift of sexuality—what God intended as a pleasurable expression of love between a husband and wife has been cheapened to the point that those who aren't distorting it are embarrassed to talk about it.

Sexual issues facing students may have become more complex, but God's plan remains simple. In fact, it hasn't changed at all since Paul the apostle challenged the Corinthian believers 2,000 years ago to remain pure.

Your students should recognize that the decision to refrain from sexual activity until marriage is actually a choice to enjoy lovemaking as God, the one who created sex and knows more about it than anyone, intended it to be enjoyed. It's not a decision based on fear or repression but on the desire for the best sex imaginable.

FYI

There are many kinds of connectedness between humans. Taken over the course of a lifetime, sexual connection is neither the most rewarding connection personally nor the most signficant connection cosmically.

Yet Paul reminded the Corinthians—who were living in a sleep-with-anyone-anytime culture that made L.A. look like Ames, Iowa—sexual intercourse is one of the more curious intercourses, because it unites two people somehow in ways that other intercourses don't. Permanently. It doesn't matter if they love each other. Their motives for having sex don't matter. Whether it's a weekend fling or a 50-year marriage doesn't matter. The union that is the result of having sex with someone, writes C.S. Lewis in *Mere Christianity*, must be endured or enjoyed forever.

Of course, the reason God wired us this way

continued on page 38

OPTION 1 S'mores—Right Here, Right Now

As kids arrive clear an area in the middle of the room and ask them all to gather around. Produce a box of campfire and S'mores supplies, and tell them you'd like to start the class off with the old favorite campfire snack.

Crumple up some newspaper, break some twigs into kindling, arrange the kindling over the paper, all the while talking about old campfire memories, asking them to tell about their favorite campfire foods and generally ignoring their amazement that you are building a fire indoors. Lay some larger logs around the kindling and start to look for some matches. The point is to make this whole

You'll need...

- campfire materials— newspaper, kindling, logs, matches, roasting sticks
- Graham crackers, marshmallows, chocolate candy bars

was to make marriage that much easier: Sex with one's spouse only ties the marital bond a little stronger. The complication comes when you make that bond, that connection, with someone you don't plan on living with for life. Those sexual ties begin pulling you in several directions, and eventually pull you apart in some ways. Perhaps this is what Paul meant when he wrote that those "who sin sexually sin against their own bodies."

scenario look like you're about to torch the place. *Do not light the fire* (duh). When it seems that you're about to light your fire, pretend to come to your senses and...

Transition into the **Tough Times** section by saying—

> Wait! Is this a reasonable thing to do? Of course it isn't! Why not? Is there a problem with a campfire? Is there anything wrong with wanting a little warmth and a few S'mores for everyone. No!
>
> The problem is that campfires were never meant to be lit in the middle of the floor. In fact campfires are wonderful things and S'mores are a great campsite treat *when they're enjoyed where they were meant to be!* Fires are meant to be enjoyed in fireplaces.
>
> This reminds me of sex. (Their first thought will be that apparently everything reminds you of sex, but go on.) It's one of the greatest things God invented, but it must be enjoyed within the safe boundaries he designed. Just as fire belongs in the safe confines of a fireplace so it won't become destructive and damaging, so sex is meant to be enjoyed in the safe boundaries of marriage.
>
> Most of us understand the dangers involved in expressing our sexuality outside of marriage. Those of us who have had the benefit of being taught in church and in our homes, should be especially sensitive to what God calls us to in these areas.

OPTION 2 Gimme Five Sexual Statistics Game

Copy and cut up the **Gimme Five** cards so that there is one set for every four students. Move your students into groups of four and distribute the cards—two to each student with the question face-up and the answer down. Instruct them not to look at the answers on the back until it's their turn and they've guessed what the answer is. Each of the questions is based on statistics found in Josh McDowell's "Why Wait?" research and explores some aspect of adolescent sexual behavior or attitude.

The idea of the game is to have each student read a question to the small group and then try to guess the answer themselves. The other students in the small group determine in their own minds if the answer should be higher (indicated with a thumb up), lower (indicated with a thumb down), or if the guess is within five percent of the right answer (indicated with an open palm down). Scoring is as follows: if the question readers guess their own answer within five percent, they get five points. If the group members are correct in their responses, they get a point for each correct thumb up or thumb down. In groups of four that means each person should get two shots at guessing and six shots at judging the guesses of others.

Transition into the **Tough Times** section by saying—

You'll need...

- a set of cards (one for every four students) cut from **Gimme Five**—Starters 4.1

It's easy to get depressed at the statistics we hear concerning teens and sex. It seems like everyone has one more statistic to terrify us with. I understand that spouting statistics doesn't solve anything, but there is one statistic that is particularly unsettling and, perhaps more than all the others, should concern you.

Say One Thing and Do Another

Many recent surveys of high school students show a sad trend. The statistics that measure the sexual behavior of adolescents show that there is very little difference between the sexual behavior of church kids and those who claim no church connection at all. Church kids will always *say* that it is very important to pursue sexual purity, but in many cases their choices don't reflect their values.

One unpublished study done at a Christian college showed 94 percent of students said that remaining sexually pure until marriage was very important. Amazingly, over half of the students who had been in a dating relationship reported having serious sexual regrets. Another study showed just a three percent difference between sexually active youth group kids and those who claimed no personal faith at all.

Ask your students if they have any idea why this might be so. If they come up blank (which is pretty unlikely) you might suggest things like we watch the same movies, listen to the same music, and read the same books. We have developed a morality that tries to avoid consequences. Rather than making choices on the basis of God's holiness, we make choices on the basis of what we believe we can get away with.

Clip tip

Jaci Velasquez has a great song called "I Promise" on her *Heavenly Place* album (Sony Music, 1996). In it she shares her commitment to sexual purity and it reinforces the emphasis of Paul's teaching very effectively.

It might also be because we make moral decisions simply so that we don't appear as bad as those with no moral compass.

DIGGING IN Small-Group Discussion

1 Corinthians 6:13-20

Explain to your students that this discussion will teach us how God feels about sexual sin and how we ought to honor him with our bodies. Distribute pencils, Bibles, and **Digging In: Sex, sex, sex,** and have your students break into their small groups for discussion.

You'll need...

- copies of **Digging In: Sex, sex, sex**—Tough Truth 4.2
- pencils
- extra Bibles

DIGGING DEEPER 1 Thessalonians 4:3-8

This passage contrasts a believer's attitude toward sex with that of an unbeliever.

On a flip chart, make two columns with headings GOD'S KID and WORLD'S KID. Use the Thessalonians passage as a starting point for your list of contrasting sexual attitudes and

You'll need...

- flip chart
- markers

behaviors. Once you have the basic points from the passage in their appropriate columns, ask if there are any other things to add from the real-life experiences of your students.

Purity Is Every Body's Business

Distribute the **Purity Is Every Body's Business** half-sheets. (Top half is for girls, bottom half for boys.) Have them write down their thoughts about each other, then complete the second statement about what they themselves could do to remain sexually pure.

You'll need...

- copies of **Purity is Every Body's Business**—Tough Choices 4.3, cut into halves (girls get top half, boys get bottom)
- pencils
- copies of **Psalm 139**—Tough Choices 4.4

When they've finished, collect the cards and read the responses. Challenge the guys to hear what the girls are saying and the girls to hear what the guys are saying. Remind them that sexual purity is a choice and that they should start with themselves.

Realize that some of the students in your class are probably living with some significant sexual regrets.

Extra effort

If the schools in your community provide abstinence education, make the effort to call those in charge and let them know of your support. Check to see if they have any resources available to help you in your teaching on the subject of moral purity.

If your community does not have such a program in the schools, explore the possibility of forming a committee of concerned citizens and doing what you can to make it available to your students.

Make sure to talk about sexual purity in a way that gives them hope from here out. Remind them of God's forgiveness and his willingness to give people a new start.

Close your session by having everyone read Psalm 139 responsively or in unison from *The Message.*

Memorize this important idea from one of Paul's other letters.

For God did not call us to be impure, but to live a holy life. (1 Thessalonians 4:7)

Gimme FIVE

Make a two-sided copy of this page, then cut the cards out.
You'll have a question on one side and its answer on the back.

What percentage of guys have had sexual intercourse by the end of their teen years?

What percentage of teens who said they have had intercourse said that they only did it once?

What percentage of college women say they have been raped or sexually attacked since they were 14?

What percentage of 11- to 13-year-olds say they are sexually active?

What percentage of teenage girls who get pregnant are pregnant again within two years?

What percentage of high school students feel that abortion is the best solution for a pregnancy?

What is the percentage by which teenage sexual activity and pregnancy has increased since condoms have been made available to high school students?

Of teens who marry while they are pregnant, what percentage will be divorced within five years?

Starters 4.1

Gimme FIVE
2nd side

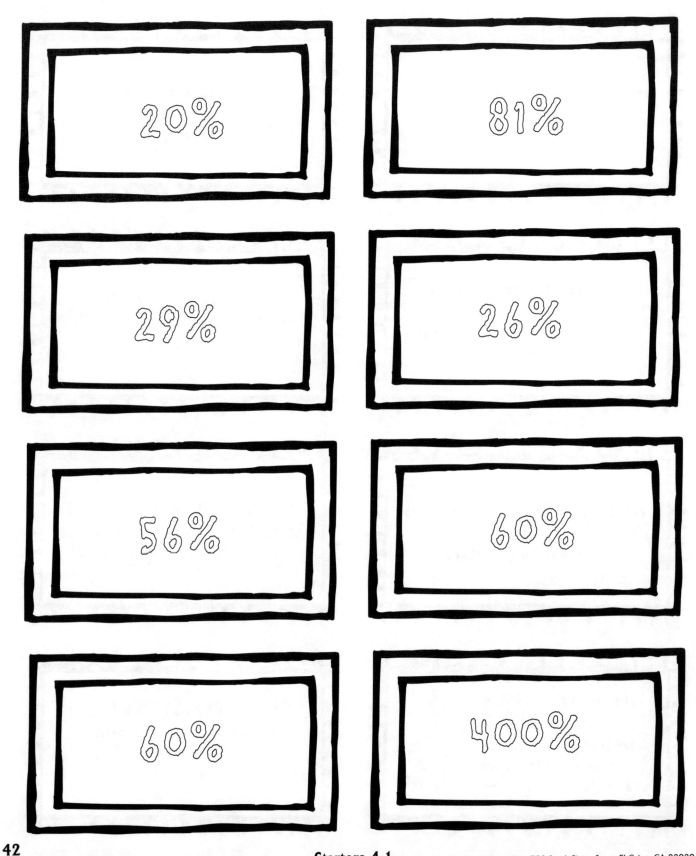

20%

81%

29%

26%

56%

60%

60%

400%

Starters 4.1

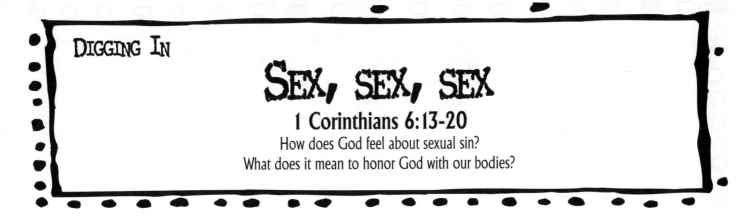

SEX, SEX, SEX

1 Corinthians 6:13-20

How does God feel about sexual sin?
What does it mean to honor God with our bodies?

1. Corinth was a city filled with sexual temptations. What are some everyday places where the topic of sex comes up?

2. We talk a lot about sex being one of God's good ideas. If you were God, would you have done anything differently in the design of human sexuality?

1 Corinthians 6:13-15

3. Paul says that our bodies were made for the Lord. What does he mean by that?

4. Name some ways you can use your body to honor God.

5. Why do you suppose the urge to sin sexually is such a strong temptation for people your age?

6. If we were able to see our bodies the way Paul describes them in these verses, what would we see?

7. How does this high view of our physical bodies change the way we make sexual decisions?

1 Corinthians 6:16-17

8. This verse talks about a guy and a prostitute. Is sexual temptation just an issue for guys? Is there a principle here that applies to girls as well?

9. The Bible says in several places that when two people have sex, they become one flesh. What do you think that means?

10. According to the "one flesh" principle, what happens when people have sex with several or many partners before they are married?

11. Read verse 17 again and talk about what happens when someone who is spiritually one with God becomes physically united with someone in a relationship that breaks God's rules.

1 Corinthians 6:18-20

12. The first part of verse 18 is pretty straight-forward. What are some other words you could use for *flee*?

13. Think of some actual choices teenagers could make in their everyday lives if they wanted to flee from sexual immorality.

14. Look at the last half of verse 18. How is sexual sin like shooting yourself in the foot? Before the *therefore* in verse 20 Paul says five things about us and our bodies. What are they?

15. According to the verses we've looked at today, what should be our main reason for choosing to stay sexually pure?

Tough Truth 4.2

PURITY IS EVERY BODY'S BUSINESS

WHAT GUYS COULD DO TO MAKE IT EASIER FOR GIRLS TO STAY SEXUALLY PURE:

WHAT I COULD DO TO BE SURE I STAY SEXUALLY PURE:

PURITY IS EVERY BODY'S BUSINESS

WHAT GIRLS COULD DO TO MAKE IT EASIER FOR GUYS TO STAY SEXUALLY PURE:

WHAT I COULD DO TO BE SURE I STAY SEXUALLY PURE:

Tough Choices 4.3

Psalm 139

GOD, investigate my life;
    get all the facts firsthand.
I'm an open book to you;
    even from a distance, you know what I'm thinking.
You know when I leave and when I get back;
    I'm never out of your sight.
You know everything I'm going to say
    before I start the first sentence.
I look behind me and you're there,
    then up ahead and you're there, too—
    your reassuring presence, coming and going.
This is too much, too wonderful—
    I can't take it all in!

Is there anyplace I can go to avoid your Spirit?
    to be out of your sight?
If I climb to the sky, you're there!
    If I go underground, you're there!
If I flew on the morning's wings
    to the far western horizon,
You'd find me in a minute—
    you're already there waiting!
Then I said to myself, "Oh, he even sees me in the dark!
    At night I'm immersed in the light!"
It's a fact: darkness isn't dark to you;
    night and day, darkness and light, they're all the
    same to you.

Oh yes, you shaped me first inside, then out;
    you formed me in my mother's womb.
I thank you, High God—you're breathtaking!
    Body and soul, I am marvelously made!
    I worship in adoration—what a creation!
You know me inside and out,
    you know every bone in my body;
You know exactly how I was made, bit by bit,
    how I was sculpted from nothing into something.
Like an open book, you watched me grow from
    conception to birth;
    all the stages of my life were spread out before you,
The days of my life all prepared
    before I'd even lived one day.

Your thoughts—how rare, how beautiful!
    God, I'll never comprehend them!
I couldn't even begin to count them—
    any more than I could count the sand of the sea.
Oh, let me rise in the morning and live always with you!
    And please, God, do away with wickedness for
    good!
And you murderers—out of here!—
    all the men and women who belittle you, GOD,
    infatuated with cheap god-imitations.
See how I hate those who hate you, GOD,
    see how I loathe all this godless arrogance;
I hate it with pure, unadulterated hatred.
    Your enemies are my enemies!

Investigate my life, O God,
    find out everything about me;
Cross-examine and test me,
    get a clear picture of what I'm about;
See for yourself whether I've done anything wrong—
    then guide me on the road to eternal life.

From Eugene Peterson's *The Message: The New Testament in Contemporary Language*

45

Tough Choices 4.4

SESSION 5 MYSTERIES OF MARRIAGE

1 Corinthians 7

HERE'S THE DEAL

Healthy marriages grow on biblical principles.

THE BIG PICTURE

Marriage is the Rodney Dangerfield of institutions. It gets no respect. Try finding an accurate, realistic portrayal of healthy married life on the tube. Chances are you'll be clicking through the channels for a long while.

It's always been this way, of course. Anything that promises as much intimacy as marriage does is bound to be exploited. Or sought by shortcut. Which usually short-circuits the relationship altogether. Ancient Corinthian culture went this way, much of the modern world is going this way. Yet St. Paul's model of matrimony—exclusive monogamy or absolute celibacy—is a model your students have quite possibly never heard presented as serious options, not to mention as fulfilling and very satisfying ways to live.

This lesson helps your students recognize that marriage is not something to be taken lightly (nor is singleness, for that matter). The relationship between a husband and wife is demanding and complex—which is reason enough to build a marriage according to God's design and purpose.

FYI

You get the feeling that in Corinth, sex was in, marriage was out. Yet when the city's citizens believed in Christ and joined the church and tried to put their hedonistic lifestyle behind them, it appears they overreacted. Not only did they stop visiting the temple prostitutes (this was good), but they suspected that any sex—and even marriage—was somehow wrong (this was not good).

Enter Paul the Marriage Counselor. Marriage has its burdens, he wrote—one of which is that you spend more time cultivating your spouse and the marriage itself than you spend cultivating your relationship with Christ. That's not bad, Paul wrote, it's just the fact of the matter.

Other marital facts and advice from Paul, from 1 Corinthians 7:
• Be content as you are, single or married. If single, it's fine to marry. If married, stay married—

continued on page 48

JUST FOR STARTERS

OPTION 1 Media Marriage Models

Group your students in twos or threes, pass out a **Media Marriage Models** sheet and pencil to each group, and give them two minutes to brainstorm and write down as many TV marriages as they can (for example, Homer and Marge, Fred and Wilma, the Huxtables, the Bradys, etc.). After two minutes ask two groups to get together and score their lists. Don't be too picky about getting the names exactly right—the "Mad About You" couple, Paul Reiser and Helen Hunt, or the Buckmans would all be fine. They get one point for every marriage their

You'll need...

• copies of **Media Marriage Models**— Starters 5.1
• pencils

even to an unbeliever who is content to stay married to you.

• If you are not compelled to remain celibate, then for heaven's sake marry. God loves married people no less than celibates. It's just that they love him back in different ways.

• Husbands' and wives' bodies belong to each other, not just to themselves. Corollary: if you're married, don't deprive your spouse of sex (unless you both agree, and for only a while)—the temptation is too great otherwise.

partner group didn't have.

Once they've scored their lists, ask them to discuss the three questions listed on their sheets for each marriage the two groups had in common.

After their small-group discussions, ask the whole group:

• What would you say is the most realistic marriage portrayed on TV?
• What is the healthiest marriage on TV?
• What are the signs of health you see in that marriage?

Transition into the **Tough Times** section by saying—

> We see a lot of marriages on television and in the movies. Some are healthy, most aren't even close! We see the marriages of our parents and the parents of our friends. Again—some of them are healthy and some are disastrous. A lot of us have made decisions about how we'll handle marriage someday. Remember that the challenge of marriage is to have a *healthy* relationship, and the Bible has some very practical things to say about how that can happen.

OPTION 2 Whose Kids Are These, Anyway?

You'll need...

• someone with morphing software and a scanner
• pictures of the kids in your youth group
• a method of displaying the images from the software as described below

You might be able to find someone who has a computer graphics program that allows you to morph photographs. The software basically animates a smooth transition between two different photographs that you've scanned. Somewhere in the middle of the transition, the image is a 50/50 blend of the two photographs. These blended images can be captured and shown on a computer screen or printed for kids to see.

For larger groups the printed images can be photocopied onto color transparencies at a copy shop and projected so everyone can participate. The idea of this opener is to morph the pictures of pairs of kids in your group and let everyone guess "whose kids they are" (for example, "Here's what the kids might look like if Jennifer married Bob"). After the kids get the idea, have them guess the original couples when they see the blend. It might be fun to start with some celebrity morphs—the pictures are readily available on the Internet—and then move into some pictures of familiar faces to end the opener.

Transition into the **Tough Times** section by saying—

It seems like some things about marriage are predictable—we assume that if the cheerleader and the quarterback got married they'd have great-looking, athletic kids. We imagine that the couple in our group that seems so in love today will be passionate for the rest of their lives. We assume that one day our prince (or Sleeping Beauty) will come and that, like in all the fairy tales, we'll live happily ever after.

Two Thumbs Up for Marriage

You'll need...

- a transparency made from **Two Thumbs Up for Marriage**—Tough Times 5.2

Project the controversial statements of the **Two Thumbs Up for Marriage** transparency on the wall, and ask your students to respond accordingly: give an enthusiastic two thumbs up if you strongly agree, one thumb up if you sort of agree, two thumbs down if you really disagree, and one thumb down if you sort of disagree. Note there is no neutral option.

As your students agree or disagree with each statement, select several who are giving two thumbs up or down and give them 30 seconds each to make their point. Don't feel like you need to get the "right answers"—I'm not sure there are any—simply allow the students to express their thoughts as a way of preparing them for the lesson to follow.

DIGGING IN Small-Group Discussion

1 Corinthians 7

You'll need...

- copies of **Digging In: Married in Corinth (or in Cleveland)**—Tough Truth 5.3
- pencils
- extra Bibles

Divide your students into groups of three or four. Ask half of the groups to name five benefits of being married, ask the other half for five benefits of remaining single.

After they have had a few minutes to discuss the benefits of the position you've given them, move them into new groups where two from each perspective are represented (i.e., two from the promarriage group get with two from the pro-single group). Have them try to persuade each other that their position is correct. It will be kind of an informal debate.

Next, distribute **Digging In: Married in Corinth (or in Cleveland)**, pencils, and Bibles, and have them discuss the questions in their discussion groups.

Clip tip

There's a great song in the video *The Wedding Singer* (New Line Productions, 1998) called "I Wanna Grow Old with You." You must preview it if you intend to use it—chances are most of your kids have seen it, but a line or two might be considered a bit over the edge. It's the romantic cry of a man in love. Use it at your discretion.

DIGGING DEEPER Ephesians 5:22-33

This classic passage on marriage relationships is rich with symbolism and meaning. For the purpose of this study it will be viewed from just one perspective.

Read the Ephesians passage, then put your students in small groups of all guys and all girls. Give each of them a large piece of paper and some markers. Have the girls write down as many adverbs (words ending in *ly* like freely, sacrificially, etc.) as they can to describe how Christ loves us. Have the guys write down as many adverbs as they can to describe how the church loves Jesus. Have each group pick four of its words, move kids into coed groups, and have the girls tell the guys how a husband could show a wife the four kinds of love they've selected. Give the guys the opportunity to do the same for the girls.

Extra effort

Invite four or five couples to come answer questions about marriage. Pick couples who have been married for varying lengths of time—perhaps one in the first five years, one between 10 and 15, one in the 25- or 30-year range, and one around 40 or 50 years. It would probably be wise to avoid parents of students in the group to minimize the embarrassment potential.

Decide whether you'll take written questions on 3x5 cards or if you'll just let the kids ask their questions directly. The written method might give you a little more honesty in the questions. Emcee the proceedings inviting responses from all the couples and keeping the discussion moving. Wrap up the panel by allowing each couple to share a sentence or two of prepared advice for your students who might need it sooner than they think.

A Letter to the One I'll Love

A lot of us have dreamed about what marriage will be like someday. Some people even create a list of qualifications or characteristics they're looking for in a marriage partner. Ask your students if any of them have ever thought of such a list. If they have, let them share some of the things on their list. If not, have them think of some of those things now.

Affirm the thoughtful responses then say something like—

Often when we think of marriage we think about what we will get from it—companionship, sex, the undivided attention of someone who cares deeply for us, a partner who will bring out the best in us, etc. Have you ever thought about it from the other angle—what your partner will get when he or she marries you?

Distribute copies of **A Letter to the One I'll Love** and then give your students a few minutes to write a letter—maybe their first ever—to the person they will marry. The letter is a chance to tell their partner what *they will bring* to marriage, the commitments they are making right now to prepare to be a husband or wife, the character qualities they are working to develop, and their understanding of what it will take on their part to make a lifetime marriage work.

Memorize this Old Testament teaching that Jesus quotes.

For this reason a man will leave his father and mother and be united to his wife, and the two will become one flesh. So they are no longer two, but one. (Mark 10:7-8)

Media Marriage Models

As a group, list here as many TV marriages as you can in two minutes:

Get with another group, and cross off the names you have in common. You get one point for every marriage the other group didn't have on its list. Write your score here:

Still working with the other group, list below those marriages that *both* groups thought of. Explore these questions about those marriages.

Marriages	What about this marriage is like real life?	What about this marriage is totally unlike real life?	What chance would you give this marriage in the real world?
			Divorced within a year • • • • • • • Married for life
			Divorced within a year • • • • • • • Married for life
			Divorced within a year • • • • • • • Married for life
			Divorced within a year • • • • • • • Married for life

Starters 5.1

Two Thumbs Up for Marriage

Women usually have to give up more than
men to make a marriage work.

A marriage with no children can't be as
healthy as one with kids.

According to the Bible, the man is
the head of the house.

Opposites attract—and
usually have the best marriages.

God has one person selected for each of us
and it's our job to find that person.

A good goal for a husband and wife is to
eliminate conflict from their home.

The ideal arrangement is for moms to stay
home and care for the kids.

Marriage is a thing of the past; in a few years
it won't be a part of our culture.

Most marriages could last a lifetime
if people just worked at it.

Tough Times 5.2

DIGGING IN

MARRIED IN CORINTH (OR IN CLEVELAND)

1 Corinthians 7:1-5, 10-24, 29-34

In this chapter you'll find biblical principles for a healthy marriage. It's only one of many biblical passages about marriage, so you really need to read more than just this passage to get the big picture, the accurate picture. Still, Paul gives some very practical advice here. The Corinthians—new Christians, you remember, who had until recently run with the wildest in a wild city—were apparently making up their own rules about marriage. This is a long chapter, so we'll explore only a few of the verses.

1 Corinthians 7:1-2

1. Paul wastes no time giving his opinion on the debate you just participated in. What is it?

1 Corinthians 7:3-5

2. You should know that in Paul's culture ownership meant responsibility. You had to care for the things that belonged to you. How does that information help us understand verses 3-5?

1 Corinthians 7:10-24

3. How would Paul feel about the easy divorce standards we have in our world today?

4. Verse 14 makes it sound like as long as someone is married to a believer they are made pure because of it. Is that what this verse means?

5. How does a godly wife help her ungodly husband to become godly?

6. Verses 17, 20, and 24 all give the same principle. What is it?

7. What can we count on from God when he calls us into something?

1 Corinthians 7:29-31

8. What is Paul thinking? Doesn't this sound awfully harsh?

9. Why does Paul say we ought to live with such focus and discipline? Is it the same for us today?

1 Corinthians 7:32-34

10. These verses talk about some of the issues you raised in your debate at the beginning of this discussion. What advice would you give a married couple who really wants to please God with their lives? Is it possible to be committed to God and be happily married?

Tough Truth 5.3 Copyright Youth Specialties, 300 South Pierce Street, El Cajon, CA 92020.

A Letter to the one I'll love

Tough Choices 5.4

1 Corinthians 8

FYI

You know the issues that generate strong pro and con feelings among a church's members, or between members of neighboring churches. Home school versus public school. Christian school versus public school. Homeopathy versus antibiotics. Rush Limbaugh versus NPR. Youth group dances. R movies. Raised hands in worship services. Wine with meals.

What threatened to divide Corinthian Christians was this question: should they buy meat that had been an offering to idols, then (because of course the idols never consumed it) was put out on the butcher's discount shelf: PORK LOIN, DAY-OLD IDOL MEAT, 50% OFF. Don't touch that stuff, said some—this meat was spiritually tainted by pagan ritual. Hey, it's a great deal, said others—the idol is no god, just wood or stone. (Can you hear in this disagreement modern Christians' arguments for

continued on page 58

Sometimes you need to shelve your Christian freedom for the sake of others.

What good is freedom if a person can't exercise it? That's

the tricky question facing all Christians. Yet along with the freedom that God's grace brings comes responsibility. Yes, we are free to do any number of things, but we have a responsibility to make sure that no one else suffers because of our freedom. Welcome to the infamous Gray Areas of Christian life.

You may have no problem—or you may have a huge problem—with knocking back an occasional brewsky with friends after a sweaty softball game. Or with renting an acclaimed movie whose R rating is due to a single instance of the f word. Or clearing out the chairs in the church sanctuary to make room for a step class of women and men dressed down in leotards or shorts. Scripture doesn't specifically endorse or prohibit these activities. It's up to us to determine how we feel about it.

In making those determinations we are obliged to look beyond our own freedom. Where is the line at which our legitimate freedom in Christ begins actually chipping away at the faith and confidence of another believer? What was true for the Corinthians 2,000 years ago is true for us today: the choices we make affect other people. What is harmless to one can be harmful to another—especially if the other has been raised in a different background with a different set of beliefs. Your students should understand that Christian freedom allows them to make many, many choices for themselves, and if push comes to shove, Christian love compels them to defer to Christians less mature than themselves.

OPTION 1 Mobile Moves

This opener illustrates the effect one person can have on a community.

Divide your group into teams of five to seven, and ask students to think of an adjective that starts with the same letter as their first name and describes them well. You'll have Funky Frankies, Sassy Susans, and Marvelous Marys all over the place.

Distribute supplies and have them decorate a 3x5 card with their new name on one side and the number of years God has been part of their lives on the other side. Have them work as a group to create a mobile that hangs all their name cards in balance.

Hang the completed mobiles from the ceiling and then use one to make your point. Move one of the cards by pulling on it. Immediately all the cards in that mobile begin to will move. Say something like—

When Gorgeous George here, who has had God in his life for nine years, decides to make a move, what happens to Perky Patty who has had God in her life for one year? Of course, George's move affects her and all the others who are connected.

OPTION 2 Video Clip

Show the clip from the movie *Liar, Liar* (Universal City Studios, 1997) where Jim Carey's character pulls his son out of Kindergarten to get permission to lie again. You'll find it at 42:42 into the movie and it begins with Carey's character looking into the Kindergarten classroom window. The clip runs about three minutes until the teacher calls the class in from recess.

Set the clip up by explaining that the boy made a wish (the night before at his birthday party) that for just one day his dad wouldn't be able to tell lies. The wish came true, and now the dad doesn't know how to function. The point that our freedom to do something can powerfully affect the people around us is clearly illustrated.

As always, when you use a video clip, be sure to preview it, have it cued up right, and know when you'll stop it.

Regardless of the opener you chose, transition into the **Tough Times** section by saying—

We talk a lot about our personal rights these days—"I do whatever I want to do and it's nobody's business but my own, just between me and God." But is it that simple? We often ignore the fact that some of the lifestyle decisions we make can profoundly

affect our walk with God. We can easily forget how what we do affects people around us as well. There's no doubt that Christ has provided us with a freedom that was unheard of in the legalistic systems of the Old Testament. Christ freed us from the law, but with that freedom comes an awesome responsibility to use our freedom for the growth of those around us.

Trapped or Free

Use the **Trapped or Free** page to illustrate that some areas of our lives that we consider neutral aren't neutral at all. Those areas have great potential to be expressions of our freedom in Christ, or potential traps slowing our walk with him or tripping up people around us.

Have students examine each of the things down the middle of the page. Ask them to write down a specific way in which they could be trapped by it and also a way they could use it to enjoy freedom in Christ. They'll see that a lot of things that appear to be neutral just aren't!

You'll need...

- copies of **Trapped or Free**—Tough Times 6.1
- pencils

DIGGING IN Small-Group Discussion

1 Corinthians 8

Begin the discussion by explaining the dilemma faced by Christians in Corinth.

The city had many pagan temples where sacrifices to idols and false gods occurred. Once the sacrifice was done, the meat could be sold for food, so there was always a fresh supply. The Christians were a little uptight about eating this meat, because they knew what it had been used for and were afraid of possible punishment by God.

Distribute pencils, Bibles, and **Digging In: When there's no black and white**, have the students get into their small groups, and discuss.

You'll need...

- copies of **Digging In: When there's no black and white**—Tough Truth 6.2
- pencils
- extra Bibles

DIGGING DEEPER Hebrews 12:1

Ask for three volunteers to compete in a quick timed competition against the clock. Call contestant 1 to the front and have her put on a pair of hockey gloves or several layers of mittens and gloves. Tell her to write the words of Hebrews 12:1: "Let us throw off everything that hinders and the sin that so easily entangles." Time the effort and post the resulting page. Have contestant 2 do the same thing. Again, time it, and post the result. Have contestant 3 come up and prepare as the others did, but just before he begins to write, let him take the gloves off. Obviously his time will be better and his writing more legible.

Ask your students if there is any relationship between what they just saw happen and the words that were being written. The lesson is simply this—you can either wear gloves or take them off, but if you want to write so others can read, you'll choose to get rid of the gloves.

Notice there are two categories of things to get rid of—only one of them is sin. The other category is simply those things we choose to eliminate so we'll grow and not trip up those around us.

Tough Calls Decision Tree

Walk your students through the **Tough Calls Decision Tree**, then have them work through it using a dilemma they're in right now. Encourage them to carry this handy little tool in their Bible or school notebook until the process of making decisions becomes second nature.

Close in prayer thanking God for the freedom he gives us in Christ and asking him for the courage to live responsibly within that freedom.

Memorize

this thought Paul wrote to the Roman church.

So don't condemn each other anymore. Decide instead to live in such a way that you will not put an obstacle in another Christian's path. (Romans 14:13, NLT)

FYI cont.

and against observing Halloween?)

In Rome, meanwhile, the issue was simple vegetarianism. Christians with a strong Jewish background just couldn't shake the feeling that some foods (meats, in this case) were simply not right to eat, and that some days were holy days and ought to be observed as such (see Romans 14).

Paul understood that some new Christians couldn't shake their pagan associations overnight. Eating meat that had been offered to idols was the same to them as the practice of idolatry itself. And when they observed more experienced Christians scoop idol meat off the bargain shelf, they were inclined to wonder if, just maybe, eating such meat was okay after all. Maybe they were being too squeamish. With the result that new Christians ended up buying and eating idol meat ("It must be okay if the Smiths eat it—and *they're* strong Christians"), but they felt terrible about it.

Paul, as usual, let love—charity—be the decider. The burden, he wrote, was on stronger Christians to suck it up and forego eating idol meat *if* eating idol meat caused spiritual confusion among new, less mature Christians. Not that there was a thing wrong with the meat, Paul pointed out. Meat's meat, and idols are nothing. But if eating perfectly acceptable meat means wounding another's weak conscience, Paul wrote, he'd stop eating meat forever.

Notice that Paul did *not* write that he'd give up meat because another Christian merely *disagreed* with his eating it—but only because the faith of the other Christian was undermined by it. Notice, too, that Paul calls Christians whose faith can handle eating idol meat *strong*, and those who cannot eat it with a clear conscience *weak*. Seems to contradict the stereotype of Christians who are "good" because of what they *don't* do.

Trapped or Free?

How could I be trapped by this area of life?

How could I enjoy my freedom in this area?

food

friends

sports

TV

money

movies

the Internet

sleeping

education

exercise

Tough Times 6.1

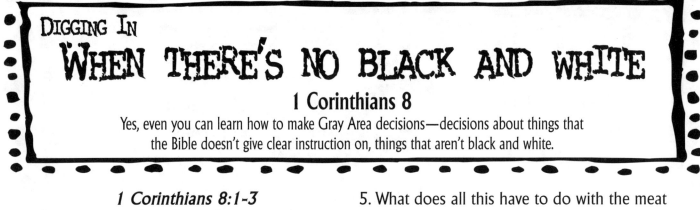

DIGGING IN
WHEN THERE'S NO BLACK AND WHITE
1 Corinthians 8
Yes, even you can learn how to make Gray Area decisions—decisions about things that
the Bible doesn't give clear instruction on, things that aren't black and white.

1 Corinthians 8:1-3
1. Paul starts out by talking about attitudes. Summarize what he says.

2. The topic Paul is about to address is quite controversial. Some people aren't going to like what they hear. Why does he address the attitude issues first?

1 Corinthians 8:4-7
3. Who are the people Paul is really concerned about here?

4. How does Paul compare idols with the true God?

5. What does all this have to do with the meat issue?

6. Think of some things in our modern culture that would raise the same sort of questions for new believers. (Hint: Something from your past life that might be a point of weakness for you.)

1 Corinthians 8:8-13
7. If Paul is saying in verse 8 that this is no big deal, what is he saying in the rest of the chapter?

8. Mark an X at a place on the line that describes your feelings about these details of 21st-century living.

How free am I about seeing R movies?	Free as could be —— Never watch 'em
Odds of weakening the tender faith of another Christian?	Pretty good chance —— No chance
How free am I about listening to sexually explicit music?	Free as could be —— Never listen to it
Odds of weakening the tender faith of another Christian?	Pretty good chance —— No chance
How free am I about missing church?	Free as could be —— Never miss it
Odds of weakening the tender faith of another Christian?	Pretty good chance —— No chance
How free am I to hang with friends who are drinking, though I'm not?	Free as could be —— Never do it
Odds of weakening the tender faith of another Christian?	Pretty good chance —— No chance

9. Finale: what would you be willing to give up for the sake of protecting a weak or new Christian from falling back into sin?

Tough Calls Decision Tree
Should I?

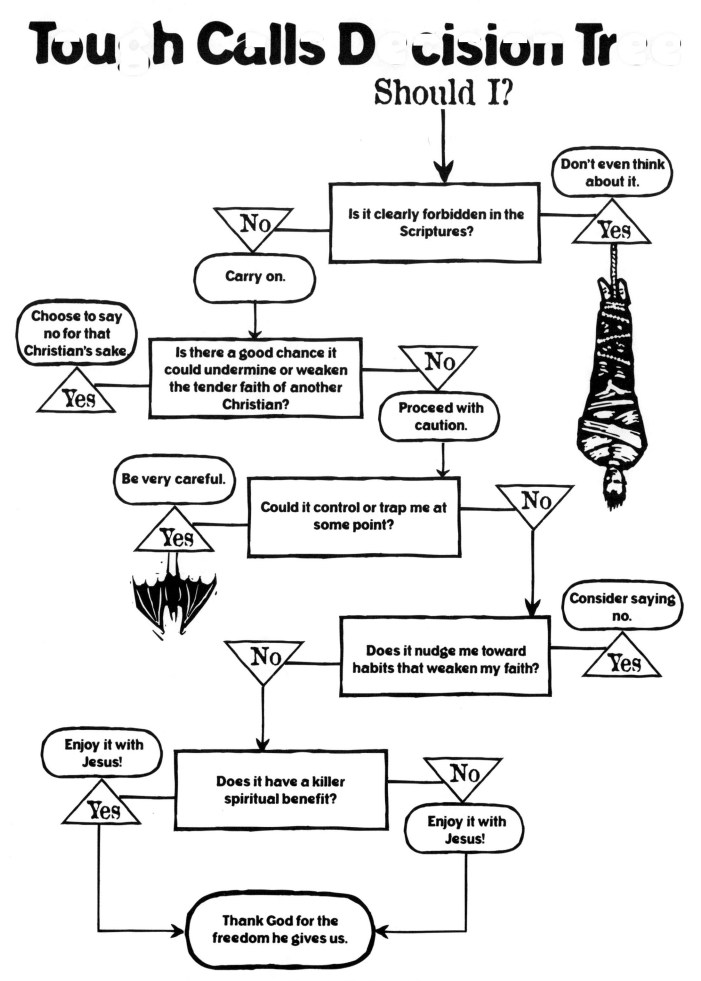

Is it clearly forbidden in the Scriptures?

No → Carry on.

Yes → Don't even think about it.

Is there a good chance it could undermine or weaken the tender faith of another Christian?

Yes → Choose to say no for that Christian's sake.

No → Proceed with caution.

Could it control or trap me at some point?

Yes → Be very careful.

No

Does it nudge me toward habits that weaken my faith?

Yes → Consider saying no.

No

Does it have a killer spiritual benefit?

Yes → Enjoy it with Jesus!

No → Enjoy it with Jesus!

Thank God for the freedom he gives us.

Tough Choices 6.3 Copyright Youth Specialties, 300 South Pierce Street, El Cajon, CA 92020.

GIVE ME A HAND LEND ME YOUR EAR

1 Corinthians 12:12-27

HERE'S THE DEAL

Believers should work at eliminating attitudes and behavior that hinder their unity with each other.

THE BIG PICTURE

When it came to capturing people's attention, Jesus was right up there with the best. Chatting with an individual or addressing a crowd, our Lord knew exactly what to say or do in order to communicate his message in the most effective manner possible. And what advice did he give his followers more often than not? Some version of this: if you want to draw people's attention to your changed life as a Christian, get along with each other. Jesus knew that the sight of his followers working together for a common cause would be a more powerful testimony to his life-changing message than any sermon or personal witness.

It sounds simple enough, this unity-with-other-Christians stuff—but it's a chore. And it's a frequent subject in the apostle Paul's pair of letters to the Corinthians. His practical suggestions for functioning as one body address issues that still plague believers today. If your students struggle with self-centeredness, competitiveness, pride, or fear, they will find Paul's advice especially helpful.

JUST FOR STARTERS

OPTION 1 Some Assembly Required

The idea of this opener is to illustrate to students that each part is important. Bring several Walkman-type personal stereos to class or ask several of your students if you can borrow theirs. (You'll need one for every five students.) Each unit should break down into five separate parts (two batteries, headphones or detachable speakers, basic Walkman unit, and cassette or CD). Put each part into a small, brown paper bag.

As students arrive, give them a bag and instruct them not to look inside. Ask them to move quickly and randomly into groups of five, unpack their bags, and make some music. Chances of a complete unit showing up in one group are slim. Have them put their components back into their bags and put together new groups of five.

FYI

First, the subject: "spiritual gifts"—gifts from God for the people of God, for "the common good" of the church. St. Paul's Greek word for "gift" here is *charisma*. (The Greek word for "grace" is virtually the same word, *charis*, which shows you what a gift *that* is.)

Second, the facts: here are the primary (and possibly the only) passages in the New Testament that list spiritual gifts as such:
• **1 Corinthians 12: 4-11.** Here St. Paul lists *ability gifts.* Open your Bible now, and read the list.
• **Romans 12:3-8.** Here's a similar list of ability gifts, explained by Paul for Christians in Rome.
• **1 Peter 4:10-11.** A brief mention of a couple ability gifts, this time by the apostle Peter.
• **Ephesians 4:7-16.** Look out—here's a turn in the road. These gifts are *people gifts*—people, rather than abilities, that God gives to a community of believers.
• **1 Corinthians 12:28.** We end up in the same chapter we started in, only at the end of the chapter. Here Paul begins his list with people gifts (apparently in some kind of first-second-third order), only to switch midlist to ability gifts.

Finally, a clear, definitive explanation about

continued on page 64

You'll need...

- one personal cassette or CD player for every five students
- a brown paper bag for each student

FYI cont.

what spiritual gifts look like today and how to put them to use "for the common good": Ha-ha. Christians have batted this one around since the Council of Chalcedon tried to pin down the nature of Christ, and with no more luck. Following are only some of the questions that are up for grabs, although many churches and denominations officially endorse one interpretation or another:

• **Does God still distribute spiritual gifts today? If so, which ones? If only some, why not the others?**

• **Why does it seem that a church's endorsement of *some* spiritual gifts and not of others is less a question of theology, and more a question of comfort level?**

• **What is the interplay, if any, between 1) your spiritual gift, and 2) your talents, skills, and expertise that came your way thanks to heredity, upbringing, and training?**

• **How do you determine your spiritual gift?**

In any case, one gets the feeling that we've made this spiritual-gifts thing a lot more complicated than it is.

After several attempts at random groupings they will start to look around and see what other people have in their bags and cooperate to ensure that their group has everything it needs to put their complete musical units together. When everyone has their units assembled and running, point out that being the person with the Walkman didn't make them any more important than being the one with the batteries. Remind them that having the CD or cassette was pointless without having something to play it in. With even one piece missing it was impossible to use the unit as it was intended.

OPTION 2 Balloon-Bursting-Body-Part Relay

You'll need...

• a large room
• uninflated balloons
• several chairs

This very active relay is something of a youth ministry classic, but if your kids haven't seen it, you can have some fun with it. You'll need a bigger room than some youth groups meet in and some clear space for people to run.

Identify two or more teams of five people to become "bodies" as follows: two strong guys are the legs, a girl they can carry is the mouth, a guy or a girl is the hand, and finally (and here's where you can have some fun) a guy to be the rear end. Put the bodies together at the front of the room—the two "legs" forming a seat between them for the "mouth" to sit on, the "hand" linking an arm in the "mouth's" arm, and of course the "rear end" behind. At the back of the room locate an assistant for each team to wait with a balloon. Clear a path between the "body" at the front and the balloon holder at the back.

The object of the game is for the entire body to run to the back of the room so the hand can pick up the balloon and hold it so the mouth can inflate it. When the balloon is inflated the body runs back to the front of the room where the hand holds the balloon on a chair or on the floor so the rear end can sit on it and burst it. The first popped balloon wins.

OPTION 3 Puzzling People

You'll need...

• full-body pictures of people from magazines cut as described in Option 3

Here's a simple and quick opener. Find magazine or catalogue pictures of people whose arms, legs, and heads are visible. Cut the pictures up so that each has six pieces (two legs, two arms, a head, and a body). If your group is small give several random pieces to each student. For a larger group make sure everyone has one piece. When you say "Go" have them assemble the pieces into their intended bodies.

Regardless of the opener you chose, transition into the **Tough Times** section by saying—

It's pretty obvious that unless each part is in place and doing its job, things don't work the way they're supposed to. A band with nothing but five bass players would sound pretty lame, a baseball team with nothing but outfielders would have a pretty lousy season, and a bike with no pedals would only work downhill—you'd hope the brakes were there wouldn't you?

The idea of working closely together is something Paul talks about with his friends in Corinth. It seems like they were having a bit of trouble understanding that every person in their church had an important role to play. Instead of working together, they were tearing each other apart. I wonder if we ever do the same thing in our group?

Rub Off on Each Other!

You'll need...
- flip chart
- markers

Draw a line down the center of your flip chart and, with everyone participating, brainstorm some of the contrasting categories kids put each other in. Start by writing GUYS on one side and GALS on the other, then guide them to other categories. Include positive and negative categories (for example, cool versus geeks, rich versus poor, smart versus dumb) and categories of personality (outgoing versus quiet, thoughtful versus impulsive, analytical versus emotional, etc.).

Next, look down the list and ask the students to mentally put themselves on one side or the other in each category. Is there any value in associating with people who are on the other side of the line from us in some of these areas? Ask the group to think about how their lives could benefit by connecting with someone across the line from them in several specific areas (for example, "For those of you who are outgoing, what is the value of hanging out with people who are quiet and thoughtful? And for those of you who are quiet and thoughtful, what can you gain in a friendship with someone who is more outgoing?").

DIGGING IN Small-Group Discussion

1 Corinthians 12:12-27

Explain that today's discussion will teach us how important we are to each other. Pass out pencils, Bibles, **Digging In: Look how important we are to each other!**, and have students break into their small groups for discussion.

You'll need...
- copies of **Digging In: Look how important we are to each other!**—Tough Truth 7.1
- pencils
- extra Bibles

DIGGING DEEPER John 17:20-26

Jesus prays this prayer just moments before he is arrested and eventually crucified. Can you sense the passion as you read it?

Have students work in pairs to write a prayer for unity that they would like to see prayed for your youth group or your church.

When the students are done writing their prayers, have one representative from each pair pray the prayer out loud. If you have a large group, put them into groups of eight so they can share in four prayers as a group.

You'll need...
- paper
- pencils

TOUGH CHOICES

Celebrate the Body

Before your meeting fill out the **Our Body'd be No Body without You** certificates to affirm the unique contribution each of your students makes to your community of believers. Fill in the certificates with their names and your comments in a brief sentence (don't get flowery and elaborate with this).

You'll need...

- Completed **Our Body'd be No Body without You** certificates—Tough Choices 7.2

During your meeting, ask students to think of one person in the group with whom they don't feel well connected. Help them understand that there are many reasons this might be so. Perhaps it's someone they just haven't gotten to know; it may be someone who goes to a different school, is a different age, or is new to the group. Maybe it's someone who intimidates them or makes them feel inadequate. Of course it could be someone with whom there has been conflict or competition rather than love or cooperation. Ask them to take a minute to pray silently for that person, thanking God for the contribution the person makes to the body and asking God for an opportunity to get to know that person better.

Conclude your time together by affirming each student verbally as you pass out the certificates you completed earlier.

Clip tip

Illustrate how many people it takes to make a movie by running the credits of a popular video. Point out some of the less significant-sounding roles (key grip, best boy, stunt coordinator, etc.) and help them see that everyone has an important role in the final product. For extra fun do a little quiz based on the names and roles listed.

Some suggestions:

- Thanks for being a voice for our body. You speak on God's behalf wherever you go, and it is a real encouragement to all of us.
- Thanks for being feet for our body. Your willingness to go with the good news of Jesus into places where others haven't gone is an encouragement to all of us.
- Thanks for being the eyes for our body. Your ability to see where we ought to be going and to share your vision with us all is such an encouragement to all of us.
- Thanks for being the ears for our body. Your gift is listening without being judgmental or giving pat answers, and it's a real encouragement to us all.
- Thanks for being the hands for our body. You serve us all with your attitude and actions of servanthood and we want you to know what an encouragement that is to all of us.
- Thanks for being the smile for our body. Your sense of humor brings us joy and keeps us balanced. You are an encouragement to all of us.

After distributing your affirmation certificates, comment on either the good balance you see or on any gaps you have noticed (for example, "We have a lot of voices in our body and not a lot of hands and ears. Let's pray that God will bring people into our body who will have an ability to serve and to listen").

Memorize this mandate to the Philippians from Paul.

Do nothing out of selfish ambition or vain conceit, but in humility consider others better than yourselves. (Philippians 2:3)

Extra effort

If you have any doctors, physiotherapists, or other health experts available to you, have them come in and talk for five or 10 minutes about how the body functions as a unit as described in the metaphor Paul uses in 1 Corinthians 12. The idea is to illustrate the interconnection of the many parts. Have them talk about the important roles of some of the apparently less significant parts of the body.

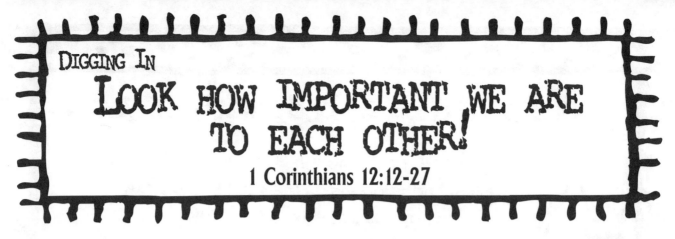

LOOK HOW IMPORTANT WE ARE TO EACH OTHER!

1 Corinthians 12:12-27

1. Think about our church (or our youth group) and describe all the forms of variety and diversity you see in the people there.

1 Corinthians 12:12
2. Why is the body a good picture of the church?

3. What are some other things that Paul could have used—things that are one unit, but are made up of many different kinds of parts?

1 Corinthians 12:14-17
4. What problem in the church is Paul addressing here?

5. Have you ever wished there was something about your personality that you could change? Complete the following sentence: "I often wish that I was more..."

6. Think of someone who is very different from you, yet you're really glad they're part of our body. Share this person's contribution with the rest of the group.

1 Corinthians 12:18-21
7. What word would describe the attitude of the eye or the head in verse 21?

8. What happens to our sense of community when people display that kind of an attitude?

1 Corinthians 12:22–25
9. Think about your physical body for a minute. What are some parts that you could live without? We're still not sure what the tonsils and appendix do, but other than those two, think about how your life would change if you were to lose even a small part of your body.

10. Read verse 23. What kind of people in the body of Christ is Paul talking about when he says that some are *unpresentable* and need to be treated with a kind of modesty (protected from view)?

11. Verse 25 gives us two goals for the body. What are they? Are these valid goals for a group of Christians?

1 Corinthians 12:26-27
12. What are some traditions we have (or could have) to rejoice with members of our group who are being honored?

13. What are some ways that the group has shown you that they hurt when you were hurting?

14. Let's give our body a quick examination. For each area give an example of how you've seen the body being healthy:
- How's our heart for people outside the church?
- How are our eyes at seeing needs in our community?
- How are our lips at speaking honestly with one another?
- How are our mouths at praising and worshipping God?
- How are our ears at listening to the needs of our friends?
- How are our hands at unselfishly serving others?
- How are our feet at taking God's good news outside of our church or group?

Tough Truth 7.1

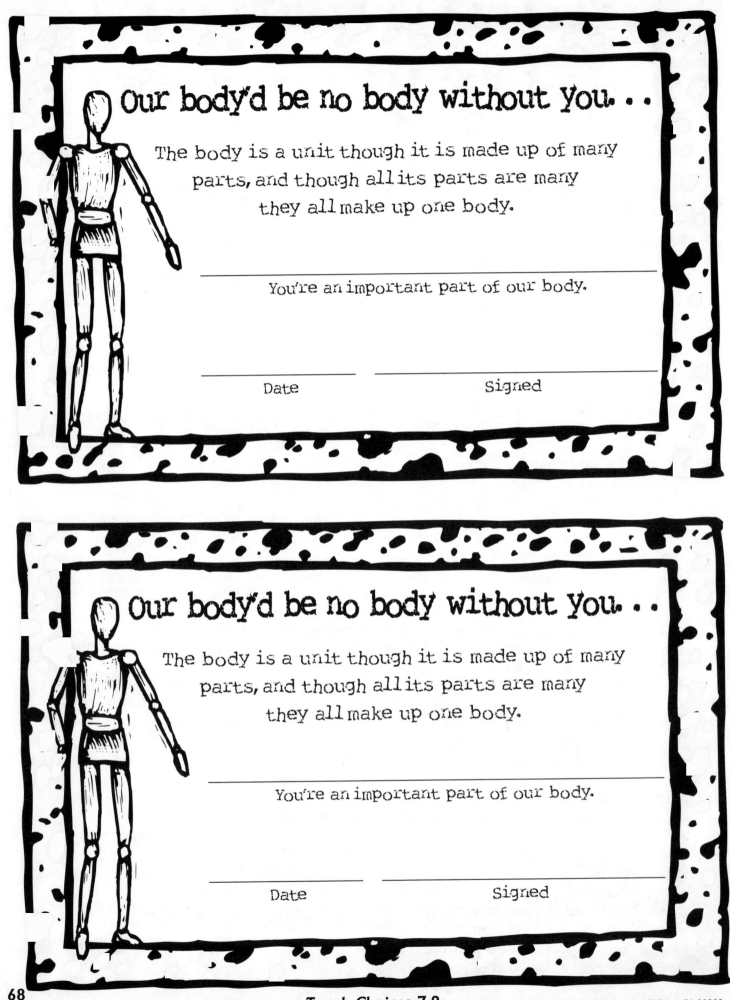

Our body'd be no body without you...

The body is a unit though it is made up of many
parts, and though all its parts are many
they all make up one body.

_____

You're an important part of our body.

_____   _____
Date   Signed

Our body'd be no body without you...

The body is a unit though it is made up of many
parts, and though all its parts are many
they all make up one body.

_____

You're an important part of our body.

_____   _____
Date   Signed

Tough Choices 7.2 Copyright Youth Specialties, 300 South Pierce Street, El Cajon, CA 92020.

SESSION 8 — LOVE IS. . . .

1 Corinthians 13:4-8

HERE'S THE DEAL

Time to separate fact from fiction about the kind of love we need to give and receive.

THE BIG PICTURE

Put some roses in a vase, light a few candles, and crank up the Kenny G.—and let's talk about love. Not just any kind of love, mind you. About genuine, biblical love—the kind of stuff that earned 1 Corinthians 13 its nickname: the Love Chapter.

On second thought, forget the roses, put the candles away, and turn the CD off, because the love we're talking about has very little to do with romance. No Hallmark sentiments here—we're talking about the kind of love that demands hard work, sacrifice, and vulnerability. It's not the kind of love you feel, it's the kind you do. The kind of love Jesus modeled. Someone once said that if Jesus had loved the way most of us do, he would have lived to a ripe old age. By dissecting Paul's timeless description of love in 1 Corinthians 13, your students learn how each element may be applied in their relationships with their friends, their family members, and God.

JUST FOR STARTERS

OPTION 1 Lovin' Life Bingo

This opener will illustrate how broadly we use the word *love*. Distribute the **Lovin' Life Bingo** cards and turn your students loose to find people who fit the categories. Determine on the basis of your group size how often you'll let each

You'll need...

- Lovin' Life Bingo cards—Starters 8.1
- pencils

person sign. Don't make it too easy. Require at least two lines before they call BINGO. Give a prize of some candy hearts to the winner.

OPTION 2 Sure You Do!

You'll need...
- plain paper
- pencils

This activity will work better with a smaller group and is less rowdy than Option 1. Distribute paper and pencils and have your students think of three things they love and one thing they don't like at all. Have them go to the front and tell the group (dishonestly) that they love all four of the things on their list. The object of the game is for the group to decide which one of the four is a lie. You can go first to demonstrate the concept. If you need some ideas, look at the **Lovin' Life Bingo** card—Starters 8.1.

Regardless of the opener you chose, transition into the **Tough Times** section by saying—

> We talk pretty casually about the things and people we love. If we really understood what it meant to love biblically, we'd probably be more cautious about using the word in conversation. Today we'll see what the Bible says about love and how that could change the way we relate to one another. Real love goes way beyond little cupids and romantic music. It will test the commitment of the toughest of you guys and the most determined of you girls here today.

TOUGH TIMES

Luv

You'll need...
- flip chart
- markers

Using your flip chart, have your group brainstorm as many popular song titles that contain the word *love* as you can. They should be able to think of at least 15 or 20. Next, look at the list and ask your students to define love on the basis of what the songs say. "What's this musician's definition of love?" If there's a video for the song, "How is love portrayed visually?"

It seems like everyone wants to talk about love but there's a lot of confusion about what it really means. Let's look at a familiar passage in the Bible that defines love in very practical terms.

TOUGH TRUTH

DIGGING IN Small-Group Discussion

1 Corinthians 13:4-8

You'll need...
- copies of **Love Is...Isn't...Does... Doesn't**—Tough Truth 8.2
- pencils
- extra Bibles

This discussion will teach us what real love looks like in action.

Begin by reading 1 Corinthians 13:4-8 in unison. Be sure everyone is reading from the same version of the Bible.

Distribute **Love Is...Isn't...Does...Doesn't** worksheets to groups of two or three. Have a race to see which group can put all of the characteristics of love in the correct categories first. There should be two under *Love Is . . .* and four under each of the others. This same activity could be done much more actively by using a flip chart at the front of the room and having several teams shouting their instructions to a recorder.

Take the two characteristics under *Love Is . . .* (patient and kind) and ask students what they mean to them (for example, love is *patient* means I am willing to wait. I am willing to put off my pleasure for a while for the sake of another person. I give people a break if they don't do what I wanted them to do. Love is *kind* means I look for ways to build people up. I find ways to make people feel better about themselves, etc.).

Divide your group into thirds and have each group repeat this process with one of the categories.

After the students have completed defining the characteristics in behavioral terms, have the groups select one of the characteristics and create a short (60- to 90- second) skit that demonstrates their characteristic in use. Have them take turns acting out their skits and allowing the other students to guess the characteristic.

DIGGING DEEPER John 13:34-35

This section will involve answering two relatively obvious and two not-so-obvious questions about love in your group. (There isn't a Digging Deeper handout for this chapter.)

• How should we love each other?
• Why should we love each other that way?
• How does our love prove to the world that we are followers of Jesus?
• What are some specific ways our group demonstrates to visitors that we are followers of Jesus?

This discussion will lead very naturally into the closing **Tough Choices** section.

TOUGH CHOICES

Stop and Start Love Decisions

Distribute copies of **Stop and Start Love Decisions** and pencils. Then say something like—

During your Bible study you looked at a lot of things love isn't and a lot of things love is. But if this stuff doesn't find its way into our most important relationships, it is of very little value. Think about your friendships, your family, and your relationship with God, and identify some areas that need to be changed.

You'll need...

• copies of **Stop and Start Love Decisions**—Tough Choices 8.3
• pencils

Clip tip

The simple voice of Forrest Gump saying, "I may not be a smart man, but I do know what love is" could provide a great start to a short video clip of Forrest rescuing Lieutenant Dan in the jungle. Follow it up with a brief discussion on the kind of love that's willing to risk everything.

After they've finished filling out their worksheets, have students circle one stop decision and one start decision they will work on this week.

Memorize this tough challenge Jesus left with his disciples.

So now I am giving you a new commandment: Love each other. Just as I have loved you, you should love each other. Your love for one another will prove to the world that you are my disciples.
(John 13:34-35, NLT)

Extra effort

If you have access to a couple of video cameras and a bit of extra time, do this activity instead of the skits in the **Digging In** section. Put students in small production crews and have them prepare a 30-second TV commercial promoting a particular characteristic of love. One or two film crews can easily look after all the taping. Kids love seeing themselves on TV, and it's a great way to let them be superstars.

Lovin' Life Bingo

Instructions

1. Find people who fit in each category and have them sign their names in the appropriate squares. They may sign your sheet only once.
2. Be the first to fill two rows up and down, across, or diagonally—then shout, "Bingo! I'm the winner!" and you may win fabulous prizes and the respect of everyone in the room.

Here's some stuff I love...

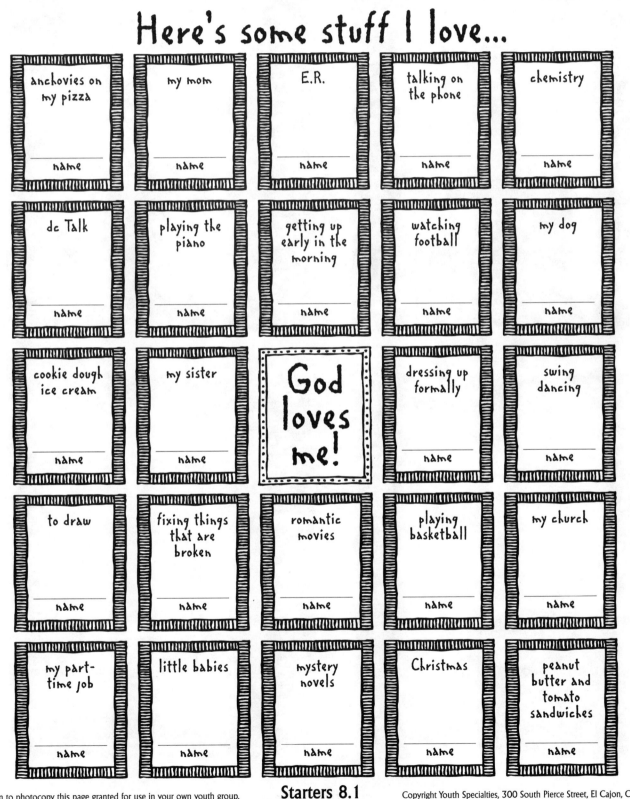

anchovies on my pizza name	my mom name	E.R. name	talking on the phone name	chemistry name
dc Talk name	playing the piano name	getting up early in the morning name	watching football name	my dog name
cookie dough ice cream name	my sister name	God loves me!	dressing up formally name	swing dancing name
to draw name	fixing things that are broken name	romantic movies name	playing basketball name	my church name
my part-time job name	little babies name	mystery novels name	Christmas name	peanut butter and tomato sandwiches name

Starters 8.1

Copyright Youth Specialties, 300 South Pierce Street, El Cajon, CA 92020.

Love Is...Isn't...Does...Doesn't

Love is...

Love isn't...

Love does...

Love doesn't...

Tough Truth 8.2

Stop and Start Love Decisions

Love is...
patient, kind, forgiving, truthful, protecting, hopeful, enduring.

Love isn't...
envious, boastful, proud, rude, selfish, touchy, score-keeping.

If I really love my friends

I need to stop being _____

I need to start being _____

If I really love my family

I need to stop being _____

I need to start being _____

If I really love God

I need to stop being _____

I need to start being _____

Tough Choices 8.3

SESSION 9 NO EASY ANSWERS

2 Corinthians 1:3-7

HERE'S THE DEAL

As badly as it may hurt now, your pain can eventually become empathy, comfort, and even healing for another.

THE BIG PICTURE

Is it viciously sentimental or just plain stupid to believe that a loving God allows tragedy and horrific trauma to happen to people? There may be another option if you believe that pain, loss, and grief can have a purpose. Not necessarily that God deliberately inflicts us with pain (we'll let your own theology wrestle with that one)—but only that your own pain, however it came to you and however deep it is, can be redeemed by God to comfort other hurting people. You can't tell someone grieving the loss of a parent or child or job or health, "I know just how you feel" unless you've already grieved through that same territory. Your words may be well meant, but they're hollow if you don't have the life experience behind them.

Sooner or later, everyone in every culture in every time experiences soul-shattering grief. It's simply part of being human. First-century Corinthian Christians did, your students have or will. And the Paul the apostle brings a reasonable, balanced, and hopeful perspective to this issue of pain. Your students will be challenged to let God use the hurt they've experienced to comfort and encourage other hurting people.

FYI

Pain gets good press these days, basically because we're closing the books on the first generation that, perhaps more than any other generation in human history, has succeeded at living pain-free lives. Anesthesia and antibiotics, after all, were used widely only in this century. Once the flu, childbirth, and cancer killed many more people, and at much younger ages, than they do today.

The pain that the Great Depression brought into millions of lives made those who experienced it vow *Never again.* Their children—boomers—have consequently experienced phenomenally little pain. They had sugar-cubed inoculations to protect them from polio and student deferments to protect them from Vietnam. Busters, Gen-Xers, and postmoderns live still in the sheltered world of the boomers. For the time being.

Which is why pain gets good press these

continued below

FYI cont.

days. It's been so rare that we're alternately frustrated and fascinated by our failure to put pain out of business once and for all. We can put a man on the moon, but we can't lick cancer. Or AIDS. Or a host of maladies that seem to descend from nowhere to kill babies, children, and adults who are loved by someone.

So how does this level with God and his supposed love for us and his supposed control of the world?

Perhaps we have been such loyal children of this age that we read into the Bible what is not there—that God will protect us from all harm and pain. The opening words of St. Paul in his second letter to the Corinthians make much more sense, yet without answering the fundamental *Why?* question, which is probably unanswerable. The God of all comfort, writes the apostle, comforts us in our troubles (Paul does not write, "keeps us from all trouble"). In other words, suffering has always sucked and will always suck—and though God for some reason doesn't protect us from suffering, he is with us in our suffering, and eventually, somehow, turns it to goodness for us and for others.

If you have ever suffered deeply, you know the paradoxical truth of this. What person cared best for your soul when you were in pain? The best healers have always been the wounded.

OPTION 1 Brain Scramblers

This activity will show your students that although answers may be tough, they're out there. Get them into groups of three or four, and let them ponder the **Brain Scramblers** page. Here are the answers so you can look real smart:

1. Her husband. (Susan's sister-in-law is her husband's sister, her mother's husband is her own husband's father, and Susan's husband is her only son.)

2. He jumped off a block of ice that was supposed to melt and leave no trace.

3. day (payday, daytime, workday, and daybreak)

4. 23 cents (2 cents per consonant, 5 cents per vowel)

5. 22

6. and (grand, gland, stand, brand, bland)

You'll need...

- copies of **Brain Scramblers**— Starters 9.1
- pencils

To summarize the activity, say something like—

> Some of these problems were tough. At first glance it might have seemed like there were no answers, but that's because the answers weren't easy. We found out there were answers, we just had to look a little harder to find them.

OPTION 2 Obstacle Course Trust Walk

You'll need...

- blindfolds for half your students
- furniture for an obstacle course

Blindfold half the people in your class, and then create a simple obstacle course with the furniture you have in the room. The individuals with sight lead their partners through the maze by giving them instructions as they go.

When they are done remind them that the reason the blindfolded people were able to get through the walk with relatively few injuries was because they had someone who could see guiding them.

To summarize the activity, say something like—

> Sometimes it seems like everything is an obstacle in life, and there's no way through it. At times like this, the only way to make it is with the help of someone whose sight is clear. Have you ever thought that you could help someone through their problems because of some insight that only you have?

Regardless of the opener you chose, transition into the **Tough Times** section by saying—

> Every one of us has, at sometime in life, asked "Why?" Sometimes our circumstances are so confusing and painful, there's no way to make sense out of them. There are just no answers. We feel alone and misunderstood.
>
> Often when the circumstances are over we find ourselves in a conversation with someone who is going through a very similar thing. It's only then that we can begin to see how God might use our painful experience and the healing we felt from him, to encourage others in their troubles.

Revisit a Painful Past

Ask your students to close their eyes. Slowly give them the following list of words and ask them to think about times in their lives when they've felt this way: ALONE, AFRAID, MISUNDERSTOOD, UNAPPRECIATED, ABANDONED, WOUNDED, HOPELESS, FRANTIC, FAILING, WEAK, CONFUSED, and HELPLESS.

Have your students open their eyes. Display the 3x5 cards where they can see them, then open it up for some of them to briefly share the circumstances that led to those feelings. Go back over the list and ask them, one word at a time, how God responds to people who are alone (is with us), afraid (gives courage), misunderstood (comforts), unappreciated (values us), abandoned (looks for us), wounded (heals), hopeless (gives hope), frantic (calms us), failing (uses us), weak (gives strength), confused (helps us understand), and helpless (helps us).

You'll need...

- 3x5 cards with the 12 feelings (listed below) written on them

DIGGING IN Small-Group Discussion

2 Corinthians 1:3-7

Tell your students that this discussion will teach us how God uses painful circumstances to prepare us to help others experiencing tough times. Distribute pencils, Bibles, and **Digging In: It hurts so bad**, and have the kids break into their discussion groups. Again, if it's possible, have adult leaders or mature students lead the discussion groups.

In the first question, be aware that many of your students will not have a dad that comes even close to the ideal dad.

You'll need...

- copies of **Digging In: It hurts so bad**— Tough Truth 9.2
- pencils
- extra Bibles

After question seven have the leaders of each small group do a little teaching. Notice the way Paul describes the process of comforting—we gain an ability to comfort others because of God's comfort in our own lives. It's not our experience of pain that qualifies us to help others. It's our experience of God that makes a difference. Talk about the danger of trying to help others out of our pain instead of our comfort. Have them close their discussion by reminding the students that God never wastes a hurt.

Extra effort

Consider starting some support groups for kids who have specific areas of hurt in their lives. There may be people in your church qualified to lead such groups, or you could tap into the resources of a community agency. For example, there's an excellent program by Alcoholics Anonymous for children of alcoholics. Call your local chapter for details. You could do the same with regional programs for victims of sexual abuse or children of divorce. At least offer the use of your church facility for these groups' meetings. What a great way to be salt and light in our communities.

DIGGING DEEPER Isaiah 9:6

Look together at this familiar Old Testament verse predicting what Jesus would be like. Have one of them read the passage after you explain that it was written hundreds of years before Christ was born. Ask them for the four descriptors of Jesus—Wonderful Counselor, Mighty (strong) God, Everlasting Father, Prince of Peace. Write all four on a flip chart, then under the titles write their responses to the following questions:

- What kinds of people go to counselors? (people who are confused, dysfunctional, unable to cope on their own, depressed, addicted)
- What kinds of people need a strong God? (people who feel weak, inadequate, and helpless)
- What kinds of people need an everlasting Father? (orphans, people whose own dads weren't there for them, people who feel they have no family, people who don't belong)
- What kinds of people need a Prince of Peace? (people who are stressed, frantic, overwhelmed, too busy, angry)

TOUGH CHOICES

A Friend in Need

You'll need...
- copies of **Letter from Jesus** stationery— Tough Choices 9.3
- pencils

Review the list of the kinds of people who need Jesus. Ask students if they know anyone who fits one of those descriptions.

Distribute copies of the **Letter from Jesus** stationery and have them write letters from Jesus to their friends who needs to hear from him. Allow some of them to share their letters if they choose but don't push it. Chances are they are pretty personal.

Memorize this instruction from Paul.

Therefore, as God's chosen people, holy and dearly loved, clothe yourselves with compassion, kindness, humility, gentleness and patience. (Colossians 3:12)

Brain Scramblers

1. Susan, an only child, was having lunch with her only sister-in-law's mother's only husband's only son. With whom was she lunching?

2. The police came into the garage and found the dead man's body hanging from the rafters 10 feet above him. He was obviously dead. There was no chair or anything near him that he could have stepped off of. "Looks like murder," said the rookie cop. "Not a chance—a creative suicide" replied the sergeant as he looked at the puddle of water under the man's feet. How did the man do it?

3. What common three-letter word fits in the blanks to create two new words on either side? (example MAIL man DATE)

PAY_____ TIME
WORK_____BREAK

4. A drugstore owner has his own way of pricing things— soap is 14 cents, shampoo is 23 cents, and toothpaste is 32 cents. How much is a hairnet?

5. What number is two more than one half of one tenth of one tenth of 4,000?

6.What common three-letter word can be added to each of the pairs of letters to make a new word? GR____, GL____, ST____, BR____, BL____.

Starters 9.1

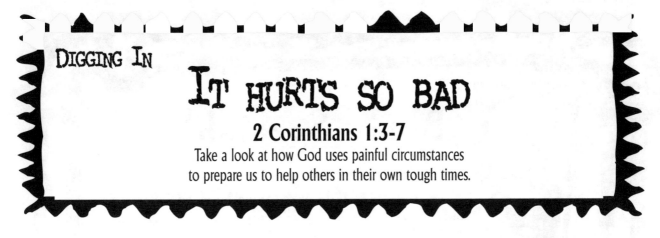

IT HURTS SO BAD

2 Corinthians 1:3-7

Take a look at how God uses painful circumstances
to prepare us to help others in their own tough times.

1. What are some words you would use to describe an ideal dad?

2. Does anyone have a memory of being a little kid, hurting yourself, and then having your dad take care of you? What did that feel like?

2 Corinthians 1:3

3. God is described here as a father of compassion. What does the word *compassion* mean to you?

2 Corinthians 1:4

4. Verse 4 starts out with a great promise. What is it?

5. List three little troubles you often experience in your life.

6. Think about yourself or people you know, and list some of the big troubles people have in their lives.

7. Why does God invest in us with his comfort?

8. What happens when two people experiencing the same sort of painful circumstances get together and neither of them has experienced God's comfort in their pain?

9. Contrast that with two people who get together when one of them has found God in the midst of it.

10. Does our pain need to be identical to the pain of the person we're trying to comfort? For example, do my parents have to be divorced before I can help someone whose parents are fighting everyday?

2 Corinthians 1:5-7

11. How does understanding this principle help Paul make it through tough times in his life? (verse 6)

12. Think of something painful in your life. Can you see a way that God might be able to use it to help someone in the future?

Tough Truth 9.2

Letter from Jesus

Tough Choices 9.3

SESSION 10 FRIENDS

2 Corinthians 6:14-18

Are non-Christian friends
a threat to your faith?

Why begin friendships that have no future? Why get
intimate with people who have very different priorities and outlooks on life than you do? Especially if Christianity is tough for you anyway, why risk having an even *tougher* time due to the influence of friends who don't understand or don't care about the life God has called you to?

The apostle Paul put these questions to the Corinthian believers, and God puts them to us today—probably because peer influence is still as powerful today as it was in first-century Corinth. So powerful, in fact, that it can turn a Christian off the path God wants for her, or help keep a Christian on that path. Some friends will consciously or unconsciously nudge your students toward God. Others will pull them away from God. And your students need to know the difference.

OPTION 1 My Imaginary Friends

Find a dozen, full-page pictures of adolescents (both guys and girls) in magazines. The idea is to display a wide range of teenage attitudes, fashions, and lifestyles—as diverse as possible. Head shots are fine, but full-body pictures would be even better. Mount the pictures on poster board, number them from one to 12, and display them where the class can see all 12.

If your group is large, have the students move around the room so they can study all the pictures. Ask them to identify three pictures that represent someone with whom they could be good friends. Move them into groups of three or four, and have them share and discuss their choices.

Follow up by asking if any of the people looked like someone they could never get close to. Again have them consider and discuss why.

FYI

Just once, you ask, couldn't the Bible say what it means—say it consistently, with no ambiguity, no equivocation?

Well, actually, when you consider that a bunch of very different kinds of people wrote the Bible's 66 separate books— sheepherders, millionaires, bureaucrats, military veterans, legal experts, commercial fishermen, half-naked prophets, CPAs—and when you think that most of them hadn't the foggiest idea that what they were writing would someday be called "the Word of God"—it begins to make sense that there's a lot of variety in the collection of history, poetry, and correspondence called the Bible.

Here we go again, you fret—what is one to make of Paul's mandate here to "not be yoked together with unbelievers" (that's not *yolk* as in egg, but *yoke* as what connects a pair of work animals to a cart or plow) when you clearly remember that this same apostle wrote the Roman Christians to

continued on page 86

You'll need...

- 12 magazine ads picturing adolescents described in Option 1
- poster board
- glue
- tacks or tape
- a marker

85

"submit yourselves to the governing authorities"? Isn't submission to government a very stringent kind of yoke or alliance? Or how about the metaphor Jesus used in his Sermon on the Mount, about how Christians should be the "salt of the earth"? If salt is to do any good, it must permeate food—at least *mingle* thoroughly with it.

So how do you refuse alliances with unbelievers, yet submit to civil authority—which occasionally *requires* you to yoke up with unbelievers? Or how do you refuse alliance with unbelievers, yet thoroughly mingle your Christian saltiness with your neighborhood, office, bowling league?

Good question. Just remember that, in the case of Jesus' salt analogy—well, it was an analogy. Jesus was making a point that even uneducated hearers could understand—he wasn't trying to wrap up all of Scripture into a neat, logical, systematic theology. And in the case of the apostle's letters to the Romans and Corinthians, remember that you're reading someone else's mail. We don't know the exact context or details of Paul's black-and-white dictates—but we do know that whatever alliances the Corinthian Christians were making with unbelievers were undoing them spiritually. One can imagine such affiliations in Corinth—or in Topeka or Portland or Birmingham, for that matter.

You'll feel it when, as you're mingling with the world—with unbelievers—you start cutting deals with your convictions. Maybe that's where mingling with the world (which is fine in itself) becomes yoking up with it (which is perilous).

FYI cont.

OPTION 2 What Makes a Good Friend Great

You'll need...

- cards cut from **Characteristics of a Good Friend**—Starters 10.1, one set for every four students
- envelopes

Before class, cut up the page of **Characteristics of a Good Friend** and put a complete set in an envelope for each group of four to five students. Ask students in each group to remove the cards from the envelope and arrange them in order of importance.

Regardless of the opener you chose, transition into the **Tough Times** section by saying—

The people we hang out with have the power to shape our attitudes and behaviors in powerful ways. Pretty much every student I know will say that their friends are the most important relationships in their lives. What a great thing to celebrate. The friendships made during the teenage years sometimes last a lifetime. We often look at friendships only in terms of what we can gain from them. This lesson will challenge us to evaluate what *we* bring to our friendships. What kind of a friend are you?

TOUGH TIMES

Pull Me Up—Pull Me Down

You'll need...

- two volunteers
- a sturdy chair

This simple object lesson illustrates the possible dangers of some friendships. Entice a muscular student to stand on the table, and a more delicate student to stand on the floor next to the table. Ask your kids how easy they think it would be for the less muscular student to push or pull the more muscular student off the chair. (Fairly easy, thanks to gravity and, if it's a chair the big guy is standing on, the narrow stance that the small seat provides). Probably a *lot* easier to push the big guy off than for the big guy to *lift* the other student up. (The lifting part of this object lesson can probably be demonstrated safely, as long as the miniature table or chair is sturdy. Make sure that the big guy you've chosen has to really work at lifting the smaller student off the ground.)

The point is simply 1) how *difficult* it is to lift up someone to your higher level, even if you're stronger, and 2) how *easy* it is to be pulled down, despite your strength. Not a bad reminder—especially for kids who are using dates as missionary projects.

TOUGH TRUTH

DIGGING IN — Small-Group Discussion

2 Corinthians 6:14-18

Digging In in this session is briefer than usual because **Digging Deeper** (below) is *longer* than usual. Just don't skip **Digging In** completely, because it's critical to what follows in this session.

Explain to your students that this discussion will teach us some of the dangers of poor friendship choices. Distribute pencils, Bibles, and **Digging In: Friends**, and have your students break into their small groups for discussion.

You'll need...

- copies of **Digging In: Friends**—Tough Truth 10.2
- pencils
- extra Bibles

DIGGING DEEPER — Selected Scriptures

You'll need...

- copies of the two-sided **The Word on Being a Friend**—Digging Deeper 10.3
- pencils
- extra Bibles

Distribute **The Word on Being a Friend,** pencils, and Bibles, and ask students to work in pairs to match the biblical friends with their "Oprah" headlines. If they look up the passages, there should be no problem.

After they've done the matching, they should turn the page over and look at the FRIENDS acrostic with its definitions of what true friends are like. Ask the students to write the names of their friends beside some of the words that describe friendship. Working through the qualities one by one, ask them to give illustrations from their friendships of each one (for example, "Can someone tell us about an experience where a friend was faithful and hung in there even when it wasn't to his advantage?"). Work through as many words as you have time for, then show your students what happens when they fold the paper back as illustrated.

Encourage them to read the seven Bible stories of friends over the next seven days.

Friendship Report Card

Distribute the **Friendship Report Card** and have students review the definitions and Scripture references for each of the aspects of friendship they studied today. Have them give themselves a letter grade in each of the categories.

Then challenge them to choose one area that needs improvement, commit themselves to working on that area this week, and write down one thing they'll do to improve in that area of weakness.

You'll need...

- copies of **Friendship Report Card**—Tough Choices 10.4
- pencils

Memorize this powerful thought from the Old Testament.

Oh, the joys of those who do not follow the advice of the wicked, or stand around with sinners, or join with scoffers. (Psalm 1:1, NLT)

CHARACTERISTICS OF A GOOD FRIEND

CARES ENOUGH TO CONFRONT

GREAT SENSE OF HUMOR

SHARES FEELINGS HONESTLY

LOYAL AND FAITHFUL

FORGIVING WHEN I BLOW IT

SPIRITUALLY CHALLENGES ME

ENJOYS THE SAME THINGS I DO

JUST A LITTLE WACKY

GENEROUS AND GIVING

A GOOD LISTENER

Starters 10.1

DIGGING IN

FRIENDS

2 Corinthians 6:14-18

Poor choice of friends can spell danger.

1. What does Paul warn the citizens of Corinth about?

2. In verse 14 Paul writes about Christians joining themselves sexually and maritally with non-Christians—to borrow a farm image, to yoke themselves together with those who don't share their faith in God. So what's a yoke, anyway?

3. What orients a Christian's life (or *should* orient it)? In other words, describe the general direction God desires for the lives of his people.

4. Now answer that same question again, but this time about *non-Christians.*

5. What do you have when two people are hooked up—intimately linked or partnered—yet moving in opposite directions?

6. Paul starts verse 17 with the word *therefore*—a big fat clue that means you've just been given a reason for something. So what's the reason for the instructions in verse 17?

7. Do you think Paul means we should have no non-Christian friends, only Christian friends?

8. Where do you think we ought to make our biggest investment in friendship?

Tough Truth 10.2

The Word on Being a Friend

Match These Friends on Oprah

Today's Guests

David and Jonathan
1 Samuel 18-23

Stretcher-Bearing Friends
Luke 5:17-26

Jesus and John
John 13:23

Barnabas and His Friends
Acts 4:36-37

Paul and Timothy
Acts 16-20

Nathan and David
2 Samuel 12

Ruth and Naomi
Ruth 1

Today's Topic

My mother-in-law is still my best friend—even after my husband died.

I'm just one of a dozen apprentices but the boss makes me feel as though he likes me best.

My best friends call me "the Encourager."

My friends renovated a house to help me get back on my feet again.

My friend cared about me enough to tell me when I was out of line.

He's still my best friend even after my dad tried to kill him!

My old friend has "bin dare and done dat." Now his letters are teaching me.

Digging Deeper 10.3

The WORD on Being a Friend

Faithful
I hang in there even when it may not be to my advantage.

> A man of many companions may come to ruin, but there is a friend who sticks closer than a brother. (Proverbs 18:24)

Risk-Taking
I choose to do things for my friends even if it hurts.

> This is my command: Love each other. "If the world hates you, keep in mind that it hated me first." (John 15:17-18)

Intimate
I let my friends know me as deeply as I know them.

> That all of them may be one, Father, just as you are in me and I am in you... May they be brought to complete unity. (John 17:21-23)

Encouraging
I look for ways to let my friends know they are valued.

> If one falls down, his friend can help him up. But pity the man who falls and has no one to help him up! (Ecclesiastes 4:10)

Nourishing
I realize that my friends need something I can offer them.

> Perfume and incense bring joy to the heart, and the pleasantness of one's friend springs from his earnest counsel. (Proverbs 27:9)

Direct
I care enough to say even the tough things to my friends.

> Wounds from a friend can be trusted, but an enemy multiplies kisses. (Proverbs 27:6)

Sacrificing
I choose to put aside my comfort and safety for my friends.

> Greater love has no one than this, that he lay down his life for his friends. (John 15:13)

Digging Deeper 10.3 Copyright Youth Specialties, 300 South Pierce Street, El Cajon, CA 92020.

Friendship Report Card

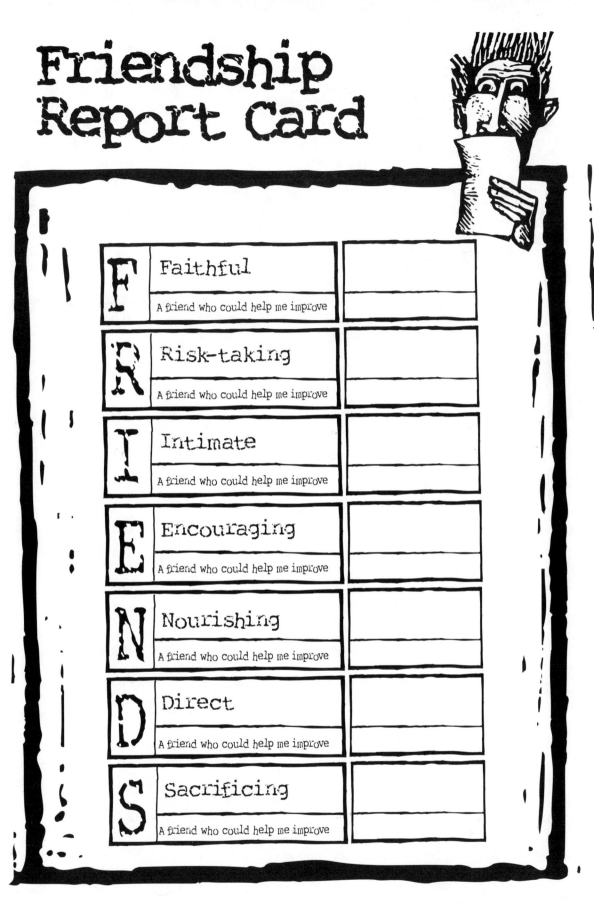

F	Faithful	
	A friend who could help me improve	
R	Risk-taking	
	A friend who could help me improve	
I	Intimate	
	A friend who could help me improve	
E	Encouraging	
	A friend who could help me improve	
N	Nourishing	
	A friend who could help me improve	
D	Direct	
	A friend who could help me improve	
S	Sacrificing	
	A friend who could help me improve	

One thing I will do to improve the area I identified as a weakness _____

Tough Choices 10.4

SHOW ME THE MONEY

2 Corinthians 8 and 9

Yes, it's still true (and still hard to do)—giving is better than keeping.

Okay, the Bible wasn't intended to be a financial guide. (*Pray and Get Rich! 10 Saintly Steps to Financial Freedom in the Here and Hereafter!*) Still, in and around everything else he talks about in his Word, God has firm opinions about the role of money in our lives. The Father's fiscal plan can be summarized in three short steps: (1) give, (2) give, (3) give.

Paul urged the Corinthians to discover the joys of being generous. Not only does God provide us with the things we need, the apostle explained, but he also gives us the opportunity to provide the things *others* need. Those who take advantage of providing for the needs of others discover that the satisfaction of giving far surpasses the thrill of ownership. What's more, givers discover that the more they give, the more they receive. It's one of those paradoxes you can't explain, but they're as plain as day once you experience them. And one of the benefits of experiencing this paradox in particular is contentment—a rare commodity among students (and adults) these days.

OPTION 1 The Price Isn't Right

The object of this game is to make more money than the competition by being a wise shopper. Read the instructions twice to make sure you understand how it works. It may sound more complicated than it really is.

Before class browse a few retail flyers and select 10 items representing a wide range of prices—a few things under a dollar, several under $5, and a few in the $10 to $20 range. Include one or two items worth several hundred dollars as well. Select items that would be of interest to your students, like junk food, video games, TVs, etc.

Cut out the ads, tape each to a sheet of paper, and cover up the price with a sticky note. Write a fictitious but believable price—either higher or lower than the actual

continued on page 96

You'll need...

- newspaper advertisements cut and pasted beforehand described in Option 1
- copies of **The Price Isn't Right Shopping List Calculator**—Starters 11.1
- pencils

95

$18.99

of the nothing they had

that, somehow, it turned into a pretty substantial cash gift for starving Jewish Christians in Jerusalem.
• Before they had given even a lira, the Macedonians had first given themselves to the Lord.
• The Macedonians gave as much as they were able—and even beyond their ability.
• Even in the middle of their own severe trials, the Macedonians' "overflowing joy" mixed with their "extreme poverty" became, with the alchemy of Christian love, "rich generosity."

Enough of the Macedonians already. Next point in Paul's fundraising appeal was to remember...
• When it comes to giving, remember the example of Jesus—who though he was rich, became poor for our sake, so that we through his poverty could become rich.
• Remember that (in the words of Eugene Peterson in The Message) "a stingy planter gets a stingy crop; a lavish planter gets a lavish crop."

And the goal of giving? A dollar amount? To go broke making a Christian organization rich?
• God doesn't want one person or church to go broke giving to another. The goal is equality—that one person's or church's plenty will supply another's need.

How much should you give?
• Individuals need to decide in their own hearts how much to give—no arm twisting, manipulation, or coercion. Whatever it is you decide to give, don't give it reluctantly or under compulsion. If you're going to give, at least give cheerfully.

And yes, there is a kickback for this kind of giving:
• After cheerfully giving as lavishly as you can, you yourself will have all you need. God promises it.

price—on the sticky note, along with a limit on how many items each team can purchase. For the cheaper items a limit of 1,000 is fine, for mid-priced items the limit should be 100, and for the highest priced items, limit them to 10. Each team can buy anywhere from zero to your limit on each item offered.

Once your meeting has begun, divide your students into teams of two or three, distribute a copy of **The Price Isn't Right Shopping List Calculator** and a pencil to each team, and let the shopping begin. Offer each item one at a time to the teams. Have them record the number of units they chose in the appropriate column.

When all teams have decided how many of each item they will buy, go back through the list and give them the actual price of each item and the amount of money earned or lost per unit. For example if you offered a CD at $9.95 and the advertised price was $11.95, your shoppers made a profit of $2.00 on every unit they chose to buy. The more they bought—the more they made. If you offered a bag of chips at $1.19 and the actual advertised price is 99 cents, they lost 20 cents on every unit they bought.

Obviously the idea is to see which team made the most money on the total differences between the actual prices in the flyer and the prices that were paid.

OPTION 2 Shopping Spree

Bring some department store catalogs, weekend flyers, and classified ads to class. Tell your students that they each have $1,000 to spend any way they'd like. Have them go through the ads with scissors and glue, and create a collage of how they would spend the money. A fun wrinkle in this project is that once something is cut out, it's no longer available to the others in the class. First come, first served.

When everyone is done, have them break into small groups and explain their collages to each other. If your group is small and the students know each other quite well, have them do their "shopping" secretly, post the "purchases," and then guess the shoppers for each collection.

Regardless of the opener you chose, transition into the **Tough Times** section by saying—

It's easy to get pretty touchy when people start talking about how we spend our money. As students we know just how many times we have to baby-sit or how often we have to ask, "Would you like fries with that?" to make a few bucks. Most of us would say that we'll be generous people someday—once we're loaded. But we must remember that habits of generosity start before we get rich and that God often gets special pleasure out of blessing people who have been faithful in little things. We're talking about money today—hold on to your wallets.

You'll need...
• catalogs, newspaper advertisements, etc.
• scissors
• glue
• paper

So Where'd All Your Money Go?

"The best way to really know a person is to look at her checkbook." Ask your students to agree or disagree and give their reasons. How people spend their money tells us an awful lot about a person's priorities, values, habits, and attitudes. Imagine that you could have access to someone's complete financial records—their credit card receipts, checkbook, investment records, paycheck stubs. What are some things you could find out about that person?

After the group has discussed the question for a few minutes, remind them that God has that view of our lives—I wonder what he sees.

DIGGING IN Small-Group Discussion

2 Corinthians 8 and 9

Explain to your students that this discussion will teach us about the joy of being generous with our money. Distribute pencils, Bibles, and **Digging In: Money** while your students break into their small groups for discussion.

You'll need...

- copies of **Digging In: Money**—Tough Truth 11.2
- pencils
- extra Bibles

DIGGING DEEPER Matthew 6:1-4

Introduce this section by telling your students that God isn't just interested in our giving, but in our attitudes while we do our giving. Jesus shoots pretty straight about how our attitudes make a difference in how he sees our generosity.

Move your students into groups of four or five. Have them read Matthew 6:1-4 and then use the bodies of their group members to create a snapshot of the two kinds of givers described. They can represent both givers in one "picture," or create two scenes to contrast the attitudes. If necessary have one member from each group explain the components of their scenes.

Debrief by asking the groups to discuss why some people find it so hard to give secretly.

If you have time, ask your students to think about this as well: most people who give to the church and other charities get a tax break. What would happen to the church if that tax benefit were removed?

You'll need...

- extra Bibles

Extra effort

Once your students have had some opportunities to be generous as a group, they will begin to experience some of the joy that comes with giving. Very few projects can provide as much satisfaction as caring for the needs of another human being. Compassion International is a reputable charity that provides for the needs of children around the world. Consider sponsoring a child (or several) as a group. Information on available programs can be obtained by calling 1-800-336-7676.

Try to get a child in a country where it might be feasible to go for a missions trip sometime. Don't talk about it until it could actually become a reality, but keep the possibility of a trip to your child's country as a possibility in the back of your mind.

TOUGH CHOICES

Puttin' Your Money Where Your Mouth Is

Ask the group to consider this question, "How could we use our money to make a practical difference in someone's life next week?" Break your students into groups of three or four, hand out copies of **Puttin' Your Money Where Your Mouth Is** and pencils, and have them brainstorm at least three ways they could give away each dollar amount (on the sheet) in the name of Jesus to make a positive difference in their church, community, or the world at large. Give ideas by reminding them of the homeless, the elderly, those in prison or in a hospital, or possible outreach areas of your church.

You'll need...

• copies of **Puttin' Your Money Where Your Mouth Is**—Tough Choices 11.3
• pencils
• 3x5 cards

When they have finished, ask the groups to share their best idea under each dollar amount. Tell them to choose carefully because next week (or at a time you specifcy), as a group, they'll actually carry out one of these ideas. Get a consensus on the group's first and second choice in each dollar amount.

Finally hand each student a blank 3x5 card, and tell them that this project (to be carried out next week, if possible) will be different from some others you've done. This will not be a fundraiser—no car washes or garage sales for this one. Instead you are asking each student to consider what he or she will give to the project. Encourage them to think about giving with some sacrifice (for example, making a lunch instead of eating fast food one day this week). Ask students to anonymously write an amount they'd like to contribute to a collection next week. Collect the cards, do a quick calculation of the total, and let them know the results. Then choose the project they'll do next week based on the dollar amount pledged. Tell them that there will be a box at the door next week for them to make their contributions.

Clip tip

Barenaked Ladies has a fun song called "If I Had $1,000,000" on their *Rock Spectacle* album (Reprise Records, 1997) that would be a great discussion starter for this topic. If you're not familiar with the band, I realize their name can be unsettling, but their music is lighthearted and fun and remarkably free from offensive material.

A note on choosing a project: Encourage the adoption of a project that involves hands-on giving rather than just sending money. For example if you decide to buy toys for the cancer ward at the children's hospital, plan a trip to take them down and hand them directly to the children. If you want to provide hot chocolate for homeless folks downtown, plan to have your students go to the streets and hand it out. It's always good for them to see their kindness making a difference.

Memorize this warning from Jesus.

No one can serve two masters. For you will hate one and love the other, or be devoted to one and despise the other. You cannot serve both God and money. (Matthew 6:24, NLT)

The Price Isn't Right
Shopping List Calculator

Item for Sale		Price	Number Purchased	Profit or Loss	Total Profit or Loss

Starters 11.1 Copyright Youth Specialties, 300 South Pierce Street, El Cajon, CA 92020.

DIGGING IN
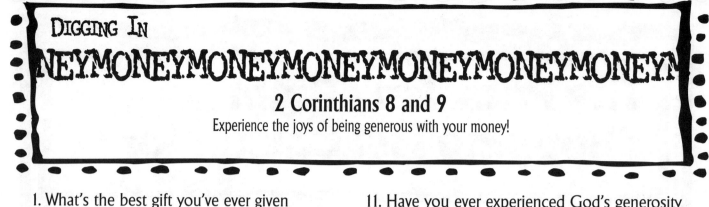
MONEYMONEYMONEYMONEYMONEYMONEYM

2 Corinthians 8 and 9
Experience the joys of being generous with your money!

1. What's the best gift you've ever given someone? What was it about giving this gift that made it special?

2. Who is the most generous person you know? Why do you think they're so giving?

2 Corinthians 8:1-5
3. How are the churches in Macedonia like the generous people you know?

4. Try to express the thoughts of verse 2 in a mathematical formula.

5. According to verse 5, what is the first step in becoming a truly generous person? Why do you think that's the case?

2 Corinthians 8:7-9
6. How is Jesus a good example of generosity for us?

2 Corinthians 8:12
7. If the amount of what we give isn't important, what is? Why does this matter more to God than the amount?

2 Corinthians 9:5-8
8. Tell us about a time when you felt pressured or manipulated to give.

9. How do you feel about the way our church deals with the issue of money and giving? Is there something we could do to be more true to the Bible?

10. What do we learn about God's character in verse 8?

11. Have you ever experienced God's generosity when you've been generous?

12. Some people say that when they give something to God, he owes them big time—like the more they give him, the more he owes them. Do you agree?

2 Corinthians 9:11-15
13. According to these verses, it sounds like when we're generous everyone's a winner. Summarize the benefits to both the givers and the receivers in the generosity cycle.

14. Are you a giver or receiver right now?

Tough Truth 11.2

Puttin' Your Money Where Your Mouth Is

$10

$25

$50

$100

Tough Choices 11.3

OUCH!

2 Corinthians 11:21-12:10

HERE'S THE DEAL

Although suffering is unavoidable, God eventually and inevitably turns it to goodness.

THE BIG PICTURE

Pound for pound, Paul may have been one of the greatest disciples who ever lived. And as payment for his faithful witness, he got roughed up a lot in the process. We're talking beatings that would make rodeo cowboys and hockey players squirm to think about. Yet Paul didn't complain much. He

understood this about suffering: even if God chose not to keep him from pain, he could count on the Lord's strength and support *in* his pain.

If your students are like the Corinthian believers, they probably aren't very good at dealing with pain and suffering. In fact, they're probably looking for instant relief from their problems. Relief may be available; an end to their problems is most certainly not. As Paul explained to the Corinthians, believers must be willing to pay whatever cost is necessary to live for Christ—and if that cost involves suffering, so be it. God will walk with us every step of the way, through everything, including pain.

JUST FOR STARTERS

OPTION 1 Lookin' Good

Distribute a set of **Lookin' Good Game Cards** to students and instruct them to make a total of 10 trades involving as many other students as possible. To trade cards they simply fan their cards out (facing themselves) and let their partner take one. Then they take one from their partner in the same manner. Do not tell students what the object of the game is. (Most of them will assume it's to end up with as many positive cards as possible.)

Let the game go on for a few minutes. Then call everyone back to order and tell your students that the cards represent a self-portrait. As a final step they can discard five cards facedown to the middle of the table.

FYI

"Suffering for Jesus," we say grimly when we hear about our pastor's mid-winter denominational conference in Orlando. "A real martyr."

(*Martyr* is an interesting word. The Greek word for "witness" is *marturia*. Those who witnessed to the saving grace of Christ during the early years of the church usually ended up on a cross or in the arena. Consequently "witness," or *marturia*, soon became synonymous with "one put to death for faith's sake," because that's what usually happened when you went public with your conversion. We English speakers, at least, have divided the one word into two: *witnessing* is testifying to your faith, *martyrdom* is the sanctioned execution of those who testified to their faith, *because* they testified to their faith.)

Actually, suffering for Jesus *is* a tricky thing. The more you hear and read, the more it seems that those whose suffering is most certainly for Christ's sake weren't all that aware of the nobility of their act. On the other hand, those who make the biggest deal about suffering for Jesus are often suffering only for their own silliness

continued on page 106

You'll need...

- a set of **Lookin' Good Game Cards**—Starters 12.1, for each student

103

Ask several people to read the 10 cards they have left.

Transition into the **Tough Times** section by saying—

> Didn't you just hate it when someone traded your good looks or respect card for the scum of the earth or being a complete loser card? We work hard at looking good to the people around us. We feel great when we have power or wealth or control. And that's interesting because from God's point of view, those are not necessarily indications of success. In fact he seems to teach us that true followers of Jesus have more than their share of grief.

OPTION 2 Name Your Pain

This is a variation of "Would you rather...?" and "What if...?" questions (lots of 'em available in book form from Youth Specialties). In this opener students are asked to decide which of two painful options they would choose if they had to. As you ask them to pick their pain, give them a chance to give a reason for their choice as well.

If you had to, would you choose to—
- stub your toe or whack your forehead?
- break an arm or break a leg?
- be stung by a bee or stepped on by a horse?
- slam your finger in a car door or freeze your tongue to a pipe?
- have the flu with throwing up or with diarrhea?
- have a canker sore on the end of your tongue or a zit on the end of your nose?
- have splinters jammed under your fingernails or a nail file jammed into your nostril?

If your students seem to be enjoying the discussion, have a few of them pose some would-you-rather dilemmas of their own.

Transition into the **Tough Times** section by saying—

> Most of us aren't great at handling pain. We work hard to keep our lives as free from hardship and inconvenience as possible. In our lesson today, we'll find that God isn't nearly as committed to keeping our lives as pain-free as we'd like. Instead he is interested in demonstrating his grace through our lives when they are marked by suffering, misunderstanding, and struggles. I know this sounds weird, but God has this thing about being closest to us when we need him the most.

Prescription Pain Relief

Distribute copies of **Prescription Pain Relief** and pencils, then say something like—

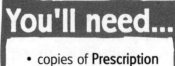

You'll need...

- copies of **Prescription Pain Relief**—Tough Times 12.2
- pencils

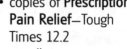

Our drug stores are lined with racks and racks of remedies for just about every kind of physical ailment there is. From headaches to hemorrhoids, there's a pill or potion for every pain. The best solutions offer *instant* relief from the symptoms.

The problem is, the deepest pain people feel is seldom physical. Look over the list of hurts and problems on your sheets, then fill in the medicine bottles with the names of the things people use (or the things they do) in attempts to make pains like those go away.

When they've completed the exercise, have some of the students share their answers.

DIGGING IN Small-Group Discussion

2 Corinthians 11:21-12:10

Introduce this section by telling your students that you'll be taking a look at Paul's life in this lesson. The man who wrote these letters and shows such concern for his friends in Corinth has lived a pretty wild and adventurous life as God's mouthpiece. It hasn't been easy.

Pass out **Digging In: In harm's way**, pencils, and Bibles, while your students break into their small groups for discussion.

You'll need...

- copies of **Digging In: In harm's way**— Tough Truth 12.3
- pencils
- extra Bibles

DIGGING DEEPER Psalm 73

Pass out copies of **Whazzup wit Dat?** and explain that in Psalm 73 the Psalmist is trying to figure out why the world seems so unfair at times—when the people who have no time for God are doing great, and the people who claim to love him are doing lousy. Ask your students to fill out the chart that shows the whole story. What you see isn't always what you've got.

Debrief the exercise by pointing out that even though the ungodly may look like they have it all together, and the godly seem confused and uncertain at times, in the end God will have the last word and his children will be the winners.

You'll need...

- copies of **Whazzup wit Dat?**—Digging Deeper 12.4
- pencils
- extra Bibles

Extra effort

Instead of using the **Prescription Pain Relief** page in the **Tough Times** section, go to a drug store and ask for empty pill bottles with labels. Fill them with jelly beans, write a pain on each label, then have students put the false solutions on the labels as well. Let your students eat the jelly beans while you explain that the solutions we often use for instant pain relief are no more effective than these candies would be for a real physical sickness.

TOUGH CHOICES

Pain Picture

You'll need...

- plain paper
- crayons or markers

Give each of your students a blank piece of paper and a crayon or marker. Tell them that you'd like to finish the session by thinking about some of the ways they and the people they know get hurt and disappointed.

Have them call out words or short phrases that describe the hurts and disappointments they've seen or experienced themselves. Be prepared to prime the pump by suggesting things like *rape, being left out, physical handicap, poverty, parents divorcing, secret eating disorder*, etc. Ask them to write down the words that are being said.

When the pages are full of words or the ideas cease to flow, stop the process and ask them to look at the list and identify any hurtful things they've experienced. Open your Bible to Hebrews 4:15-16 and invite your students to tear their pain picture into the shape of the cross as you read these encouraging words—

For we do not have a high priest who is unable to sympathize with our weaknesses, but we have one who has been tempted in every way, just as we are—yet was without sin. Let us then approach the throne of grace with confidence, so that we may receive mercy and find grace to help us in our time of need. (Hebrews 4:15-16)

Encourage them to carry the torn crosses with them for the week as a reminder that Jesus understands the hurt his children sometimes feel.

Memorize this encouragement from the heart of Jesus.

Peace I leave with you; my peace I give you. I do not give to you as the world gives. Do not let your hearts be troubled and do not be afraid. (John 14:27)

FYI cont.

or selfishness.

A couple things emerge from this passage in 2 Corinthians:

• When a Christian truly suffers for the sake of Jesus, more often than not that Christian is most conscious of suffering for the sake of another *person*. "I face daily the pressure of my concern for all the churches," Paul wrote. You get the feeling that, as he was heaving himself out of the surf and onto the beach after yet another shipwreck, he was muttering "Gotta get to Ephesus...such a young church, so many new believers, such big obstacles they're facing...," not "Gotta suffer for Jesus...anything for you, Lord...besides, this is a great example for the crew." In the big picture, of course, anything of grace we do, we do because of and for Christ. But in the crisis or the tedium of the moment, Christ looks an awful lot like a helpless child, like an irritable older parent, like an offish neighbor. "Whatever you did for one of the least of these brothers and sisters of mine, you did for me" was how Jesus put it.

• Then there's the suffering that's not imposed by a person or government, but by—well, just because we live in the world we do. Junk we just have to live with. Paul called his junk a "thorn in my flesh, a messenger of Satan, to torment me." So what was his thorn, anyway? Bible scholars have suggested physical, psychological, and spiritual maladies galore, but Paul gives us no further clue. The point was, he wrote, that 1) God did not respond to Paul's prayers for deliverance by removing the thorn, but permitted the malady to remain with him; and 2) Paul's malady was, ironically, his strength—because, as he said, "When I am weak, then I am strong."

Leave it to God to turn yet another perfectly logical idea inside out.

LOOKIN' GOOD

LOOKIN' GOOD GAME CARD

I often get beaten up by bullies.

LOOKIN' GOOD GAME CARD

People seem to like me a lot.

LOOKIN' GOOD GAME CARD

I'm the scum of the earth.

LOOKIN' GOOD GAME CARD

I've been blessed with great wealth.

LOOKIN' GOOD GAME CARD

People often call me names.

LOOKIN' GOOD GAME CARD

I get left out of most parties.

LOOKIN' GOOD GAME CARD

Most people have a lot of respect for my ideas.

LOOKIN' GOOD GAME CARD

No one ever takes me very seriously.

LOOKIN' GOOD GAME CARD

I'm physically strong and healthy.

LOOKIN' GOOD GAME CARD

Some people have told me I'm attractive.

LOOKIN' GOOD GAME CARD

God usually answers my prayers.

LOOKIN' GOOD GAME CARD

Most of the time I feel like a loser.

LOOKIN' GOOD GAME CARD

People respond well to my leadership.

LOOKIN' GOOD GAME CARD

Life basically feels like an uphill struggle.

LOOKIN' GOOD GAME CARD

My friends wish they had my wardrobe.

Starters 12.1

Prescription Pain Relief

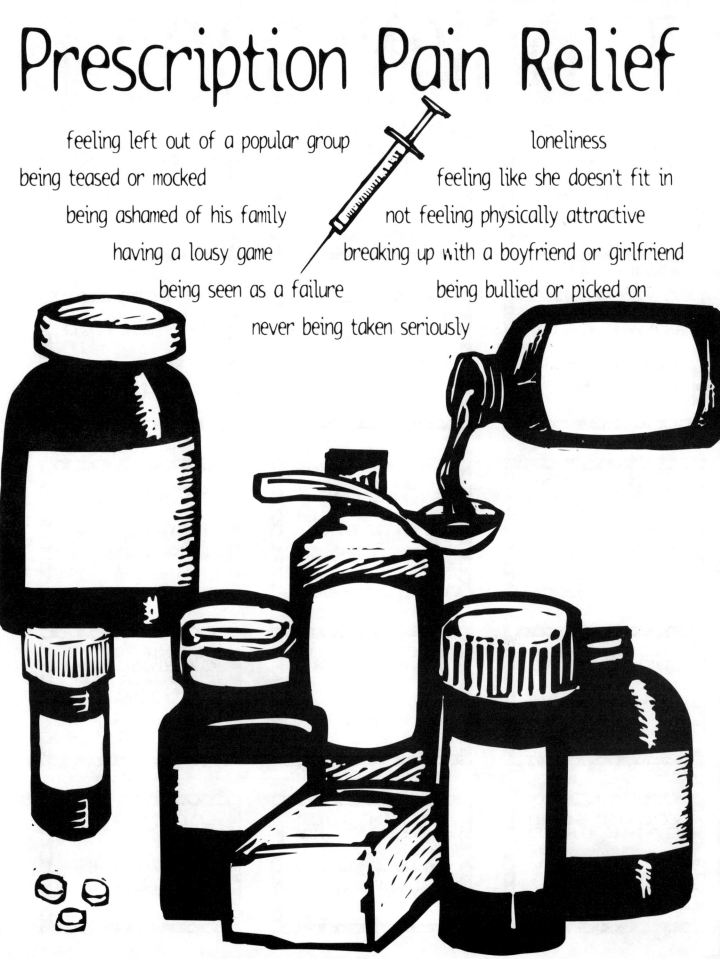

feeling left out of a popular group

being teased or mocked

being ashamed of his family

having a lousy game

being seen as a failure

loneliness

feeling like she doesn't fit in

not feeling physically attractive

breaking up with a boyfriend or girlfriend

being bullied or picked on

never being taken seriously

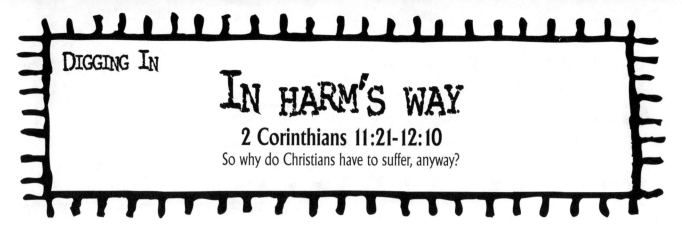

DIGGING IN

IN HARM'S WAY

2 Corinthians 11:21-12:10
So why do Christians have to suffer, anyway?

1. Has anyone here ever suffered because of your faith? Have you known anyone who has? Perhaps a missionary or a Christian in another part of the world?

2 Corinthians 11:21-33
2. Go back over the verses you just read, and make a list of all the sufferings Paul has endured for the sake of his faith.

3. What can we know about Paul's character and commitment by reading these verses?

2 Corinthians 12:7-8
4. What does Paul say is the danger of being on God's A team?

5. Verse 7 doesn't tell us what Paul's problem is, and we really have no way of knowing for sure. What is something God might do to one of us to keep us from getting too arrogant about our strengths?

6. Have you ever prayed for something and experienced God saying no? Tell us about it.

7. Did the experience of prayer answered with a no teach you anything about God?

2 Corinthians 12:9
8. God's reply to Paul's prayer is an interesting one. What is God trying to teach Paul?

9. Explain why Paul would be happy about being weak in some areas of his life.

2 Corinthians 12:10
10. List the things that Paul says he has become comfortable with.

11. Which of the words Paul uses in verse 10 describe things you've experienced for Christ's sake?

12. Think about an area of pain or weakness in your own life and take a moment to give it to God so that he can make his strength known in your life.

Tough Truth 12.3

Psalm 73—
Whazzup wit Dat?

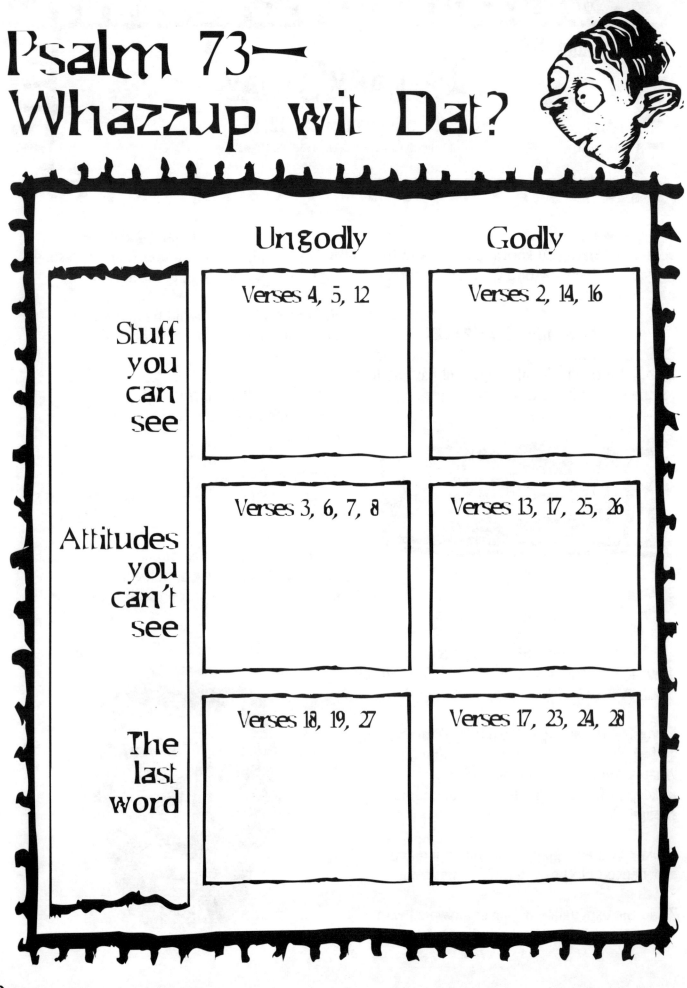

	Ungodly	Godly
Stuff you can see	Verses 4, 5, 12	Verses 2, 14, 16
Attitudes you can't see	Verses 3, 6, 7, 8	Verses 13, 17, 25, 26
The last word	Verses 18, 19, 27	Verses 17, 23, 24, 28

Resources from Youth Specialties

Professional Resources

Administration, Publicity, & Fundraising (Ideas Library)
Developing Student Leaders
Equipped to Serve: Volunteer Youth Worker Training Course
Help! I'm a Junior High Youth Worker!
Help! I'm a Small-Group Leader!
Help! I'm a Sunday School Teacher!
Help! I'm a Volunteer Youth Worker!
How to Expand Your Youth Ministry
How to Speak to Youth...and Keep Them Awake at the Same Time
Junior High Ministry (Updated & Expanded)
The Ministry of Nurture: A Youth Worker's Guide to Discipling Teenagers
One Kid at a Time: Reaching Youth through Mentoring
Purpose-Driven Youth Ministry
So *That's* Why I Keep Doing This! 52 Devotional Stories for Youth Workers
A Youth Ministry Crash Course
The Youth Worker's Handbook to Family Ministry

Youth Ministry Programming

Camps, Retreats, Missions, & Service Ideas (Ideas Library)
Compassionate Kids: Practical Ways to Involve Your Students in Mission and Service
Creative Bible Lessons from the Old Testament
Creative Bible Lessons in 1 & 2 Corinthians
Creative Bible Lessons in John: Encounters with Jesus
Creative Bible Lessons in Romans: Faith on Fire!
Creative Bible Lessons on the Life of Christ
Creative Junior High Programs from A to Z, Vol. 1 (A-M)
Creative Junior High Programs from A to Z, Vol. 2 (N-Z)
Creative Meetings, Bible Lessons, & Worship Ideas (Ideas Library)
Crowd Breakers & Mixers (Ideas Library)
Drama, Skits, & Sketches (Ideas Library)
Drama, Skits, & Sketches 2 (Ideas Library)
Dramatic Pauses
Everyday Object Lessons

Games (Ideas Library)
Games 2 (Ideas Library)
Great Fundraising Ideas for Youth Groups
More Great Fundraising Ideas for Youth Groups
Great Retreats for Youth Groups
Greatest Skits on Earth
Greatest Skits on Earth, Vol. 2
Holiday Ideas (Ideas Library)
Hot Illustrations for Youth Talks
More Hot Illustrations for Youth Talks
Still More Hot Illustrations for Youth Talks
Incredible Questionnaires for Youth Ministry
Junior High Game Nights
More Junior High Game Nights
Kickstarters: 101 Ingenious Intros to Just about Any Bible Lesson
Live the Life! Student Evangelism Training Kit
Memory Makers
Play It! Great Games for Groups
Play It Again! More Great Games for Groups
Special Events (Ideas Library)
Spontaneous Melodramas
Super Sketches for Youth Ministry
Teaching the Bible Creatively
Videos That Teach
What Would Jesus Do? Youth Leader's Kit
WWJD-The Next Level
Wild Truth Bible Lessons
Wild Truth Bible Lessons 2
Wild Truth Bible Lessons-Pictures of God
Worship Services for Youth Groups

Discussion Starters

Discussion & Lesson Starters (Ideas Library)
Discussion & Lesson Starters 2 (Ideas Library)
Get 'Em Talking
Keep 'Em Talking!
High School TalkSheets
More High School TalkSheets
High School TalkSheets: Psalms and Proverbs
Junior High TalkSheets
More Junior High TalkSheets
Junior High TalkSheets: Psalms and Proverbs

What If...? 450 Thought-Provoking Questions to Get Teenagers Talking, Laughing, and Thinking
Would You Rather...? 465 Provocative Questions to Get Teenagers Talking
Have You Ever...? 450 Intriguing Questions Guaranteed to Get Teenagers Talking

Clip Art

ArtSource: Stark Raving Clip Art (print)
ArtSource: Youth Group Activities (print)
ArtSource CD-ROM: Ultimate Clip Art
ArtSource CD-ROM: Clip Art Library Version 2.0

Videos

EdgeTV
The Heart of Youth Ministry: A Morning with Mike Yaconelli
Next Time I Fall in Love Video Curriculum
Understanding Your Teenager Video Curriculum

Student Books

Grow For It Journal
Grow For It Journal through the Scriptures
Teen Devotional Bible
What Would Jesus Do? Spiritual Challenge Journal
WWJD Spiritual Challenge Journal: The Next Level
Wild Truth Journal for Junior Highers
Wild Truth Journal-Pictures of God